PRAISE FOR

Attitude Advantage

"*Attitude Advantage: The Timeless Power of Positive Perspective* embodies the essence of leadership through positivity and resilience. Kim's expertise as a teambuilder shines through in this inspiring read, offering invaluable insights on cultivating a winning attitude for personal and professional success."

—JAMES CLEARY

Executive Vice President and Chief Financial Officer, Cencora

"I've known Kim Skanson as a friend and business colleague for many years; hers is a story of gratitude, strength, perseverance, and hope, all qualities that are a guide for success in work and life and that she shares with us in *Attitude Advantage: The Timeless Power of Positive Perspective.* This is an inspiring book that should be read more than once because it prompts you to reflect on how to take advantage of things over which you don't have control. I keep it close at hand for just those moments."

—DAVE MACLENNAN

Former CEO and Board Chair, Cargill

"Kim Skanson's *Attitude Advantage: The Timeless Power of Positive Perspective* equips its readers with the insights they need to motivate women to take control of their fates and situations and promotes ways for all of us to move forward.

There are so many great lessons in *Attitude Advantage* that you'll read it once, then pick it up again and again to keep challenging yourself as you grow."

—DEE THIBODEAU

CEO, Charter Solutions

"I have known and admired Kim for over twenty years. Great mom, great wife, baseball coach, networked professional, and standout business leader! I often wondered what her superpower was. *Attitude Advantage* shares her secrets and will help the reader develop their own superpowers."

—JEFF MADER

Retired CIO, Cancer Warrior, and Founder, CIOs Against Cancer

"I know author Kim Skanson as a caring friend and bold leader who possesses a quiet determination to succeed. After reading *Attitude Advantage*, I know how she honed these qualities of inner strength. Learning at an early age how to navigate family system adversity or drown in its wake, Kim gave new meaning to her struggles. She converted them into high octane fuel and forward momentum. In this book Kim shares her lifelong practice of Positive Mental Attitude in carefully measured doses of wisdom, insights, and life philosophies, suggesting ways we can renew and sharpen our mental edge. This book is perfectly timed given our challenging and uncertain times."

—NICK HERNANDEZ

Cofounder, Adelante Advisors, and Executive Life Coach

Attitude Advantage

Attitude Advantage

THE TIMELESS POWER
of **POSITIVE PERSPECTIVE**

Kim Skanson

Advantage | Books

Published by Advantage Books, Charleston, South Carolina.
An imprint of Advantage Media.

Printed in the United States of America.

10 9 8 7 6 5 4 3 2 1

ISBN: 979-8-89188-145-7 (Paperback)
ISBN: 979-8-89188-146-4 (eBook)

Library of Congress Control Number: 2025912062

Cover and layout design by Matthew Morse.

07-15-2025 1:35

To my grandchildren I haven't met yet.

Contents

Acknowledgments

Writing this book has been a journey of reflection, gratitude, and joy, and I could not have done it alone.

To my family—your unwavering love, support, and belief in me have been my foundation. You have taught me resilience, kindness, and the power of a positive mindset. Thank you for always encouraging me to chase my dreams.

To my friends—you are my sounding board, my source of laughter, and my safe space. Your presence in my life has been a constant reminder of the joy that comes from shared moments and genuine connections.

To my colleagues and mentors—your wisdom, guidance, and encouragement have shaped me in ways I can't fully express. Thank you for challenging me to grow, for pushing me to see the best in every situation, and for reminding me of the impact we can make when we lead with positivity.

To my mentees—you inspire me every day. Watching you embrace new challenges with courage and optimism fuels my passion for helping others. Thank you for allowing me to be part of your journeys.

To everyone who has crossed my path, offering a kind word, a moment of encouragement, or a shared belief in the power of positivity—this book is, in many ways, a reflection of you.

Special thanks to Mikaela Ashcroft for her insight, patience, and unwavering support throughout the editorial journey—her talent brought clarity and strength to every chapter.

And finally, to the reader—thank you for choosing to embark on this journey with me. My hope is that these pages uplift, inspire, and empower you to embrace positivity in every aspect of your life.

With deep gratitude,
Kim

Introduction

Inge Krieger Ibs

I don't think, when I was just starting out, that I could have imagined where I am today. I hadn't known then what I know now—a lifetime dedicated to expanding my horizons and exploring the world and myself meant one thing: a firm handshake with hard work.

Perhaps all of this started one hundred years ago, long before my own birth. A woman named Inge Krieger was born into relative privilege. She lost everything in the horrors of war but somehow managed to carve out a life for herself, traveling thousands of miles, and into a new era, to a new land and new people. Her life of ups and downs carved out a narrative, a natural way of living, that would allow anyone to turn desperate circumstances into possibilities. It took one small woman to create a vision of my future life.

Inge, my grandmother, molded my perspective on life. Though she never saw what I did, because of what she represented, I traveled the world and saw people and cultures far beyond what I would have seen in Minnesota. I learned to hold on when things got tough. I learned that, when you're in a bind, sometimes, that's the best position to be in. My grandmother was always someone I looked up to. The impossible didn't seem quite so daunting when comparing my life to someone so incredible.

Contrary to popular beliefs about the inherent value of money and its influence on leading a good life, I often find that an exemplary life is much simpler than that. It's all about attitude. A positive attitude can take you through life at a pace you could never imagine, just as a negative attitude can stop you in your tracks. Not accepting the pull that can come from outside pressures to stop in your career or family life can transform who you're becoming. And, to those people who never believed in you, your positive attitude can give you a competitive advantage you might never have expected.

Through the ups and downs and looking back at the final years of my grandmother's life, I started to really think about a life worth living. And it got me thinking: What makes this simple life extraordinary?

Through my years of hard work and struggle, I've narrowed an exceptional life down to three attitudes that, once adopted, can transform any life:

1. Overcoming adversity begins with a Positive Mental Attitude.
2. Transformation is possible at any stage of your life or career.
3. Being underestimated can be a competitive advantage.

Anyone can fall into extraordinary circumstances. History is littered with the names of people who have become famous simply because of their status. But an extraordinary life is often found in the shadows. Not everyone knows the deeds of someone who has touched countless lives, who has inspired others to reach heights they never could have on their own. Aside from the people who directly knew her, it's likely that most people wouldn't consider Inge Krieger Ibs anyone of particular consequence.

But to me, she is the picture of an exemplary life.

To remind me of the importance of taking everything one day at a time and always having an upbeat attitude, I have a pillow located in my home office with the simple letters PMA: Positive Mental Attitude.

My intention here isn't to give myself the accolades that might come from publishing a book. I have been in the spotlight, in leadership positions, for a great portion of my life, and it's not something I would consider as part of my legacy. On the contrary, I would like this story to serve as the inspiration my grandmother gave me. My mission is to raise others. Through sharing my story, I hope that someone out there can recognize a bit of themselves.

Everyone, no matter their circumstances, no matter where they came from, can live a truly extraordinary life. All it takes is the courage to find it.

1

A Glimpse of Past Uncertainty

INGE KRIEGER

The night of February 13, 1945—my brother Horst's twenty-third birthday—bombs rained from the sky. It was a night with an ethereal edge. The sky lit up like Christmas trees all over East Germany's River Elbe. A wave of planes dropped bombs onto a fiery town. Firefighters rushed to the streets from the outside areas into the city, desperate to stamp out the flames before they reached too far.

But it was all for naught.

The planes returned with more bombs, and more fires spread throughout the city. Desperate people came to the door, looking for help and a place to stay. We huddled in the basement, a refuge from the hail of fire. I handed out water to the thirsty, coffee to the cold. The coffee was made from roasted grain, as there were no beans. There had already been hardships for years, and the scarcity of resources had never been more evident.

There was quiet outside for a moment. We sat on the cold basement floor, looking up, desperately hoping it was all over. And it seemed to be.

The call for young soldiers went out to aid the bombed town of Dresden, Germany. We heard boots on the ground, muffled. Finally, there would be some relief for the already devastated city.

Then the third wave of bombs hit.

I was born in April 1926. I had such a happy childhood, with homegrown food and a backyard swing that made me giggle with joy as I swung through the air. I remember dreaming of flying far away, going higher and higher into the sky. Perhaps it was this feeling that made me yearn for a firm belief in God, an overall desire to develop a "love for all."

My life definitely wasn't easy—I struggled through the pain of sick siblings and parents—but I felt more privileged than most. God had spared me, though I lost everything on multiple occasions, and He would continue to do so.

I lived in a booming town, where stores were nearby and contained a variety of mysterious products, at least to me. My father's business grew, and my family came into some wealth. We prospered as my two brothers and I spoiled each other. At night, my father would tell stories about growing up, going to the universities, and going to war in 1914—the Great War. The days were filled with joy, and the evenings were peaceful and relaxing. Life was beautiful.

In 1933, while attending the first grade, I overheard my parents discussing the election. My parents favored Hindenburg, but it was ultimately Hitler who won. He promised a new Germany, restoring towns and building autobahns, ships, and planes. At a young age, I heard about the lives of the people around me changing for the better. Hitler hosted the Summer Olympics in Berlin in 1936 and the Winter Olympics in Garmisch-Partenkirchen. During the early days, we enjoyed going to the opera and symphonies, visiting museums, and attending art galleries.

A couple of years later, with industries booming, we left our home for something new, something bigger. Father fixed up an old villa we dubbed the "House in the Sun." We had a vegetable garden, a rose garden, and fruit trees. Father opened his shop close to home. It was a new era of possibilities.

But the good times were not to last.

In 1939, Hitler declared war on Poland and Russia. It was a time of great confusion. He had the power to blind so many to the truth. At first, we assumed he meant well, but our sentiments soon turned to horror when we realized he was sacrificing human beings.

My mother cried when she lifted the flag on the flagpole. My parents had already experienced war—the First World War—and my mother had already lost two brothers. Mother knew the devastation that war could cause, and it was happening so quickly after the devastation of the last war. We stood at the center of another possible devastation. One never knew what the next day would bring. Where would this monster lead us?

The House in the Sun was a haven located some distance from the main city of Dresden, so I was granted the small mercy of not knowing everything happening during the war.

That changed in May 1938 on my daily walk to school. I took a detour and came across the only synagogue in town burned to the ground. "Who would do such a thing?" I thought.

But it was only the start of a pattern. Circulating rhetoric included, "The Jewish people are not to be liked." Soon, their riches were destroyed: their fashion places, their cafes, their homes, their jobs. Each Jewish person was identified with the Star of David in yellow. No one had clear answers as to why. It was a slow process, but soon, the Jewish people began to disappear. Their broken shops were cleaned up and restored by others.

Yet life went on. The pressures of war put a strain on our lives, and our own home, business, and family needed attention.

Everything was quickly becoming twisted. Nothing stayed the same. Nothing was what they promised it would be. There was real fear then. Hitler's demands weren't what we had initially agreed to.

First one, then two brothers entered Germany's service. The food became rationed. Finally, my father was drafted to the Eastern Front. Both brothers came home just with injuries, thank heavens. It could have been much worse. Both told stories about the gruesome nature of war.

When both returned to the front, we were soon met with an official letter. Siegfried had lost his life. Then, officers came to the door to tell us that my other brother, Horst, was "missing in action."

There was so much chaos. My family had little, though it was more than many had. I had gone to stay with my cousin in Danzig when I heard the BBC on the radio. The Russians were progressing, and Danzig was in their line of sight. Maybe if I could get my family out, get them to Dresden. I rushed to a Red Cross train amid a sea of wounded soldiers.

We boarded the train, looking back at the city. I watched in sadness as the treasures of my cousin's home were left behind as we pulled away from the station, memories of youth and happy days left along with them. A once-beautiful place was now surrounded by gunfire. There was a strange calm in the air. The train was oddly peaceful, lulling our anxious minds into a state of fitful tranquility. We were alive, and we could help others. We shared conversations with other young, wounded people. Some of the soldiers were young Dutch boys who had been drafted into the SS under false pretenses. They, too, were helpless.

The next morning seemed hopeful. There were blue skies—a mercy.

Then we saw silver planes descending on the train. This was a Red Cross train carrying the wounded—surely, they wouldn't attack it. Yet, they came. We all exited the train in a panic and ducked quickly when someone yelled, "Hit the dirt, the ditches. Hide!" Then the hail of bullets. Some stood and ran into the open fire, trying desperately to escape the hail of bullets, only to be gunned down quickly. My family and I stayed low and, luckily, remained uninjured.

When we reentered the train, the atmosphere had changed. Why would they attack a train of mercy? It was just another example of war casualties, I reasoned.

We passed burned cities, war-torn and ravaged. How long would it be before everything we knew was lost? After so many lost lives, when would the new wave of destruction come upon us, and how long would the peace last until another barrage hit?

THE NATURE OF ADVERSITY

I often think about my grandmother's stories. It gives me a sense of peace when I think about the uncertainties that I experience. The stories were the precursors to my own life of questions. They were the stories I heard about that were followed up with words of gratitude. Life or death, war or peace—the only certainty is uncertainty.

My mother came from a comfortable family. Her father was a lawyer, but he died unexpectedly when she was sixteen years old. Life was thrown into chaos early. She had a life planned for herself. Her father had left her some money to go to college. Mom had followed a dream, though it seemed such a strange way to get started.

She had to grow up quickly, even more so when she got pregnant at nineteen with my sister. Though she expected sympathy from her mother, she received quite the opposite. Her mother disowned her when she learned of the news. All the money she had received from her father was suddenly stripped away from her, and she was told to leave her childhood home.

With nowhere to go, she turned to my father. He was a hard-working self-starter in construction. He didn't have much to his name, either. Still, they married before my sister was born and then settled with his parents in a small town in Minnesota.

His parents were kind, welcoming. They were the grandparents that I remember most, the couple that came from a war-torn Germany after World War II. My grandfather was a man of courage, able to whisk his bride from a Communist regime, and my grandmother was a never-failing stalwart of virtue. They took the young couple in because it was the right thing to do, and they showed them extraordinary love. I was born only a few years later into that household, in a small trailer house only one hundred yards from my grandparents' home.

We left that small house when I was four, moving only fifteen minutes away to a house my dad and my uncle built. The distance we moved was farther than I had grown used to, but I retained a strong relationship with my grandparents. In fact, my grandparents played a huge role in raising me.

Life was challenging for a while. We didn't have much money. We almost seemed to survive at the mercy of others.

My mom had exceptional fight in her. Everything seemed to move like a whirlwind around me. I didn't know what was going to happen. Neither of us did. Despite the disruption of having a baby, my mom finished college and became a speech pathologist. She juggled the responsibilities of motherhood with attending classes and working to pay the bills. I was young at the time, so her never-ending persistence just seemed normal to me. When she took her first position at an elementary school and helped special needs kids, it was just another extraordinary thing my mother could accomplish.

Because of my father's blue-collar work, we relied on a second paycheck from my mother and her benefits to keep us afloat. Construction work isn't always predictable, with whole months subject to seasonal fluctuations, so sometimes, my dad's paychecks just didn't cut it.

At the age of ten, I saw a rift start to form in my family. It may have been a long time coming, but that's something you don't really think about when you're young. My mother and my father divorced, and my dad moved out. My sister, who was a few years older, went with him, taking a room at his apartment ten miles away. Her ability to drive made it easier for her to move between our parents' homes. I was left without transportation in those early years. What had once been a family of four very quickly narrowed down to two. Life was very uncertain at that time; my family had split right down the middle. I still saw my sister and my dad occasionally, but it wasn't the same.

It's funny; when you're a kid, you don't really realize the state of your finances. Sure, you might realize that your friends can afford things you never could, but you never really understand the gravity of it all. But I became acutely aware of what a loss in finances meant at an early age. It was a lack of resources. I couldn't do a lot of the things my friends could. I felt a little more left out, a little more isolated. Combined with the recent rift in my family, things became more uncertain than ever. You never really know when those feelings will hit, but they always come.

WHEN CONTROL SLIPS AWAY

We often approach life believing in its simplicity. When we're children, we expect the same things out of life every day. The sun rises, family will always be there, and friends will remain the same. There's something beautiful about the simplicity we feel when we're young. It's almost like a superpower we don't recognize until we're older.

Some of the most memorable moments of my life centered around my grandparents. I was happy in their care. I felt a sense of stability and love that would have a profound impact on me for the rest of my life. I was surrounded by some of the most loving, encouraging people in the world.

At our earliest ages, we form attachments and relationships that give us the basis for our emotional and mental development. Secure, predictable relationships in childhood can lead to secure, predictable relationships in adulthood. We see the way the people around us act, whether good or bad, and mirror their styles. We adopt their coping mechanisms and imitate their social skills. Many of us learn how they learned. In some ways, there's a sense of predictability in the way that children will turn out. Everyone goes through a period of growth, of learning.

But there are times of real uncertainty in our early years.

Loss of control starts early. Childhood, when we're so vulnerable, is often the point at which we feel helpless. Our lives aren't really our own when we are very young; they revolve around the people who take care of us. When there are disruptions to the status quo, we tend to react in ways that correspond to our most base instincts. Emotional outbursts, comfort-seeking, regressive behaviors, and avoidance or withdrawal are some of our earliest responses to uncertainty. We haven't matured enough to refine the way we understand security, understanding, and adaptation. This results in a variation of responses that ruptures the tranquility of simplistic childhood curiosity.

The decisions that other people make have profound psychological impacts on us for the rest of our lives, whether for good or bad. If we feel uncertainty in our relationships growing up, we carry that with us into adulthood. Many of us feel a loss of control, helplessness, or anxiety as we grow. I'll bet that, right now, you can think of something that happened in your childhood that profoundly impacted you then and continues to have an impact on you now. Your responses may have become more sophisticated over the years, but there might still be a part of you that feels that inner child reacting with fear or similar responses.

Unfortunately, it's not something that we can absolutely avoid. All of us face some uncertainty in childhood. It's our first test that challenges us to sink or swim.

I was forced to grow up quickly. Circumstances changing at such a young age forced me to focus more on what I could do to help. My mother's quick response to create a stable environment for me gave me such courage, and it was an example I wanted to emulate. Careful observation showed me that the women in my life could—and did—control their own fates.

I often think about my childhood today. It had a profound impact on the way that I approach uncertainty. I learned from my grandmother when I was young that life can be beautiful and then change drastically. I learned from my mother the value of persistence through tough times.

There's a sense of comfort in the knowledge that my life mirrors theirs in some ways. We all grew up with beautiful childhoods that prompted us to maintain a Positive Mental Attitude. We also learned the value of hard work early on.

Though my grandmother certainly hasn't provided an exact blueprint of her life in relation to mine, I can't help but see a pattern that has been laid out. No matter where we are in life now, we can never truly predict where we'll be tomorrow. All the greatest people in history have gone through a similar season of uncertainty—usually multiple seasons. What we often fail to realize in the moment is that it isn't the struggle to overcome uncertainties that drives us to success; it is our reaction to it.

Our strength—indeed, our very success—comes from our persistence to keep going. The failures we see in life come when we completely shut down. Success is overcoming the idea that we'll always know what to do. The truth is that most of the time, we won't.

WORKING AT IT

Because of our lack of resources, I felt a duty to help out, even at the age of ten. I babysat on occasion. By the time I was eleven, I was working much more frequently. And, when I started working, I never really stopped. Because money was tight, I knew I had to work to buy clothes for school or anything else I needed. So, from that young age, I focused on what I had to do to support myself. I babysat, and I worked as a waitress, a nanny, and a lifeguard. I worked in the weight room of my school. I mowed lawns. Anything to bring in some extra cash.

Coming from a German background, I tended not to share my emotions. I worked for what I had, and that was it. There was no complaining and no ifs, ands, or buts. I did what I had to do growing up. And that's something I'll be grateful for as long as I live.

It was a surprising turn of events for me when my mother remarried a year and a half after her divorce. It caused a huge rift, almost like riding a tidal wave. The situation was tense, and the abrupt change in circumstances was unpredictable.

Perhaps that's what made it easier to spend so much time focusing on myself. I'd delve deeply into schoolwork, constantly thinking about my goal to be a teacher or a coach, something both athletic and academic. I liked playing competitively and loved the idea of helping others grow. I excelled in high school academics and sports, so combining the two seemed only natural. But when I entered college, I realized I was putting too much emphasis on the things that wouldn't take me where I wanted to go.

This was still on my mind when I took a manufacturing job during a university summer break. I took this job to pay the bills. It was simple, cut-and-dry. Manufacturing would give me a better understanding of a staple industry, a starting position that would provide me with experience and help with my business degree education. Better yet, it was at a factory close to where I grew up, making it the perfect mindless position I needed to think about my future and where I wanted to go.

I had so many jobs before this one, so the idea of hard work, especially between breaks and college, wasn't new. Still, I remember sweating the days away on an assembly line, putting spray painters together. And I worked next to a man named Sam on the assembly line. He wasn't my boss—just someone who worked beside me as I put those spray painters together. Yet he had appointed himself the de facto boss, as he'd been working at the same assembly line for years and no one matched his expertise. He was always there, working full-time. Sam knew the ins and outs of the assembly line—he was truly a senior worker—while I was just starting out. It's fair to say he knew far more than I did; that wasn't in question. But he wielded that knowledge unpleasantly.

"Hey, you're slowing us down!"

It was a phrase I heard frequently. But what could I do? I was the seasonal help, there for the summer, and it seemed like it was his job to make sure that everyone felt the same way: that he was in charge. It was a stressful enough job without worrying about upsetting Sam. I would frequently look at him, nod, and quietly think to myself,

You're here for a reason. Stay focused. You can do this. You need to pay your tuition bills.

Sam's attitude wasn't unusual. It was the typical manufacturing environment: We'd get a ten-minute break twice a day and a lunch break. Like clockwork, when the whistle blew, the line stopped. Then you'd get your lunch break for twenty minutes. At any other point, you couldn't stop working. As soon as you punched the clock, you got in line, the line moved, and so did you. I can now see the frustration Sam must have felt as someone who had been there for so long, putting up with a batch of new recruits regularly.

It was like another world, getting off work. Sure, I had done work like that my whole life, but the push to finish that job was enormous. I often came home with bad blisters on my hands, wondering for all the world if it was worth it.

Yet, I kept going back. I had to. It was only for a summer, and I needed the money.

Those of us who suffered on the manufacturing line, manning the machines and getting yelled at by Sam, seemed to stand behind a glass window whenever management came in. They walked through the factory regularly, those men in suits. The nitty-gritty operations of putting spray painters together seemed almost like a different world, and I couldn't help but notice the stark differences between management and me.

They walked through the factory, shooting grins and expressions that conveyed, "Hey, thanks for what you're doing," without the burden of opening their mouths. They were making appearances. They were there to ensure everyone knew they were in charge. There they walked, so close I could reach out a hand and touch them, yet they seemed worlds away. They never made eye contact, never looked up. It was almost as if I was caught up in the past, separated along class lines.

Looking back now, they seemed almost like a flash of black and white. They were simply there to do their duty, and there was no color in their remarks.

Even at the age of twenty, I recognized the absurdity that was before me. Management walked through the factory and talked among themselves, merely treating their employees as though they were machines. It wouldn't have mattered if I had said anything to them. I would see them walking by as Sam yelled at me, hands behind their backs and simply nodding at the work being done. Management wasn't grateful for the grunt work. They were just there to look under the hood. They were there to check the box.

They had set something off in me, though they would never know it. Not one among the series of robotic suits was a woman. Their system was flawed, like so many other systems before them, and it was a signal to me to do something about it.

Though I'd been waffling in uncertainty around the middle of my college career, this provided a strange bit of light I hadn't been expecting. The vacuum I saw in empathy and appreciation provided a light-switch moment. In my mind's eye, instead of focusing so much on the spray paint assembly line, I turned back to them, looked them up and down, and smiled.

One day, I was going to be just like them, but with one important difference: I was going to remember the people who worked for me, and I was going to thank them for what they did.

I still live near that factory. I drive by it often, as it's not far from where I live. I sometimes wonder what might have happened if I hadn't persevered through that job. I wonder what happened to Sam and the management that simply walked on by. It was vitally important for me to keep going, not because of some advice I received but because of the disconnection from people I hoped to avoid.

LEARNING TO PIVOT

I'm often overcome by just how uncertain life is. The moments in our lives that are the most difficult are often the most rewarding, though they might not seem like it in the moment.

It's also in these harrowing moments that I remind myself where I'm going, even if that destination isn't written in stone. For me, walking through the unknown is like stepping through a dark hallway. There are pockets of light and shadows cast on the floor that guide me based on where I've been. But as long as I keep my eyes up, I know I'll make my way to where I'm supposed to go.

It's natural to focus on the negative. You see it everywhere, but especially in the news. The hurricanes, political feuds, and protests all stick in our minds. They have a much more profound impact on us than the positive stories, such as stories of Good Samaritans and inspiring changemakers. Those are few and far between because they're not the focus of our lives.

Carrying that negative energy brings a sort of judgment, a certain avoidance of change. Though the nature of our circumstances won't change, our persistent opposition to the idea only makes it harder for us in the long run. It's like a weight pulling us down as we walk with heavy boots through a bog. The overwhelming darkness of negative emotions and energy pulls us down with stretching tendrils, most of which are of our own making.

That reaction to the most common parts of life is a tragedy. There's far more power in positive thinking than in negative thinking.

It's a common belief that when you get older, there are things you simply cannot change. While there is some truth to that, it's often accompanied by a staunch resistance to applying the control we do have over life. The reactions we have are our own doing. We have the power to turn bad situations into good outcomes, and it all starts with a Positive Mental Attitude, or PMA, as you'll frequently see me refer to it.

Life, as hard as it is, always provides ways to move forward.

Focusing on Control

Many are plagued by anxiety about the future. The uncertainties in your life can knock you off your feet, especially when you're feeling as though you've put forth the effort to take small, manageable steps. It's a strike at the heart of confidence. The momentum you feel fades.

As children, we often see life in terms of one great event leading to another. As we get older, we see that, sometimes, those major points in our lives were pivotal in our development but really weren't that big of a deal. That breakup when you were sixteen seemed like the end of the world at the time, but, now, it may seem like just another step you took to get to where you are. That job you lost when you were in your thirties may have seemed like the end of your professional career when, in reality, it was the push you needed to enter a field you truly loved.

You may express your life in periods, in stages, but that's not really true. There were ups and downs along the way, but your life is a consistent road filled with twists and turns and avenues not taken. The uphills are just as much a part of your journey as the downhills. The only difference is the effort you put in.

Even in the darkest parts of your life, you have at least some control over your situation: Your choice to step out of the door when it feels like your world is crumbling, your choice to let one of your priorities go in favor of another, and your choice to take accountability for a decision that hurt you all start with small steps. But that piece of your mind that lies dormant in times of stress is your saving grace. It's your key to controlling what you want despite external pressures demanding that you stay within preset limitations.

As time progresses, it becomes eerily obvious that the limitations have been coming from inside yourself all along. Often, the external voices are the manifestations of something far deeper. Blaming something outside yourself for failures or limitations is easy, but the opinions of those around you—even those closest to you—have no bearing on how high you can climb.

There are always choices. There are always points of light you can pivot to see.

Visualizing Success

That first step is the hardest.

That first acknowledgment of your ability to overcome is pivotal and sometimes the most difficult to justify.

But what if the rivers of doubt you frequently find yourself swallowed by changed from a swirl of dark water to a path to success? What if, instead of feeling swept along with the tide, you chose to feel empowerment in the way that life took you?

Sometimes, the simplest act of control you can exhibit is the belief in a successful future. At the time I worked at the factory, I didn't know which direction my life would take, but the simple belief that I would eventually take my spot as an empathetic leader served as a beacon guiding me toward a successful future.

The obstacles you face can be the starting points for your visualization of success. Seeing yourself successfully completing each step toward your goal can make it feel much more attainable. The obstacles merely become bumps in the road instead of debilitating turn signals.

Success is more about the mental rehearsal than it is about seeing your success coming to fruition. The more you see yourself as the successful product of your personal beliefs, the more you subconsciously will yourself into becoming that person. It's a mental clarification of your goals and ambitions. It's an escape from fear to confidence. It's the courage to believe in a positive outcome even in the face of the unknown.

Changing Your Mindset

My journey to success has not been an easy one. No one's has. But the periods of darkness have been punctuated by an active practice of gratitude. There's something incredibly liberating about the idea that the knowledge you have gained is far more than the knowledge you have ever lost. It's popular today to have a pessimistic perspective. In fact, it's more than easy to do so. Yet when you start thinking about what you're truly grateful for, what you have instead of what you're lacking, the world becomes much more abundantly giving.

It's easy to take the immaterial for granted. But the lessons you learn through uncertainty can carry you through your next hardship. Your challenging relationships can give you key insights into developing much stronger, more secure relationships in the future. It's not the things that change your mindset; it's the experiences.

Each new lesson, each new experience, lays the groundwork for personal growth: You're gaining wisdom from uncertainties and unlocking deeper understandings of yourself and others. Gratitude is a powerful practice that magnifies your ability to cultivate self-compassion. You're uncovering emotional tools that prepare you for continual evolution. The pieces come together when you pause in the moment to reflect on your growth.

With each moment you spend focusing on gratitude, you're developing a much greater capacity to practice self-compassion. Forgiving yourself for those mistakes, even the ones you feel have left detrimental effects on your life, gives you the tools to bounce back more quickly after every fall.

Seeing the successful transition to self-acceptance in other people can seem like a faraway inspirational story. Is it truly applicable? Is it truly something you can replicate?

Those are questions you'll continue to ask yourself for the rest of your life. It's easy to see success stories from the start and end points. There's always a happy ending in fairy tales. Yet, in the midst of struggle, it's hard to see an end in sight.

All the tools given to you by a book or the advice spoken by loved ones can seem like simple platitudes at times. There are countless ways to persevere through the unknown, and it can seem as though they're all lip service.

So, to those struggling currently, I offer one bit of advice, one thing you can write on a sticky note and paste to your bathroom mirror: *The changing tides have no bearing on me. I will always overcome.*

A POSITIVE LOOK INTO THE UNKNOWN

In 2020, during the pandemic, my life changed forever. My grandmother had died a few years earlier, and my grandfather, the man who had helped raise me, was dying in his home. I was dealing with hospice care as I stayed by his side. He had lived to the age of ninety-one, a great life. His passing wasn't overly stressful, but it was like the end of an era for me. At five in the morning on June 22, he passed away.

At five that afternoon, I was admitted to the ER.

I'd been ignoring the problems I had been having with my right arm. I'd been raised to think of others' needs first, and my grandfather had been at the center of my attention. But that day, I couldn't ignore the problem with my arm any longer.

Thinking it was minor, I resigned myself to getting it checked out at urgent care. I saw the panic in my doctor's eyes when they told me to go to the ER immediately. They thought I was having a stroke.

As I sat in the ER, I felt myself having an almost out-of-body experience. They send people here for gunshot wounds, for broken bones. Patients come here for emergencies. Certainly, I wasn't having one of those. I was exhausted, of course. My grandfather had just died. My focus had shifted. Maybe it was just an overreaction from urgent care. My body was just having an adverse reaction to the amount of time I'd spent with others on my mind.

Then my thoughts shifted. *Stay positive, Kim. PMA. You've been through tough scrapes before. You're OK; you're OK.*

I focused on my breath as they wheeled me into a CAT scan and then an MRI machine. Those breaths would have to stay in a nice easy rhythm for the next three hours.

By the time they wheeled me out, it was three in the morning. I didn't say anything, but I looked for some sort of answer in the nurse's eyes. He didn't look at me. Clearly, he knew something. Everyone who came in contact with me treated me just a little differently than they had before I had those scans. I'm pretty intuitive, and I knew that wasn't a good sign. Negative thoughts started creeping in.

As I lay in my bed, they told me the doctor would be there at seven in the morning to do rounds. He showed up at six. My first instinct was to think, *Well, I guess it must be bad. I'm the first stop of the morning.*

Without even a greeting, he asked, "Can you get your husband on the phone? Can we video conference him in?"

My heart dropped.

Their discussion took place decidedly without me. The doctor showed my husband monitors that were turned away from me. He wouldn't say anything else to me. I knew it was bad. My mind kept racing with thoughts of *It's a stroke* or *It's a brain tumor.* Whatever the case, I knew I had the support of my family, though their presence was barred by COVID-19 restrictions.

The doctor sighed before announcing the prognosis to both of us: "It's multiple sclerosis."

Multiple sclerosis (MS) is an autoimmune disorder. The body's immune system mistakenly attacks its own tissues. Specifically, it targets the protective coating that surrounds nerve fibers in the brain and spinal cord. Imagine a nerve ending as an electrical cord covered with a protective plastic coating. With MS, this coating is gradually damaged, and holes are poked through the plastic to expose the underlying nerve fibers. When those fibers are exposed, it disrupts the normal flow of electrical signals. You might lose the function of a limb or your eyes. You're in cognitive decline because your own body is attacking itself.

I felt the color leave my face as I heard the diagnosis. How could this be happening to me? These sorts of things only happen to people who aren't healthy, surely. I'm very healthy, generally, an athlete. I would sign up for a marathon on Friday and run it on Sunday even if I'd never trained. I prided myself on my consistent athletic condition. If I was the epitome of health, eating well and exercising my whole life, how could this be happening?

But MS doesn't work like that. And every journey for someone with this autoimmune disorder is different.

Today, there are a lot of drugs that can make the symptoms better. In days gone by, many would end up quadriplegic. Though it wasn't typically a cause of death, it could considerably contribute to further diseases. Today, it's not necessarily a death sentence. But it is life-altering. I'll never have a normal path through life. Someday, I may lose sensation in parts of my body, and there's no cure. It's like hearing a cancer diagnosis, but the practitioner says it's not going to be too bad. But someday, it's going to take you. It will always be in the back of your mind.

I returned to the life list I'd always kept. What did I want to do that I'd never done before? What did I want to learn? How did I want to live if a lack of physical mobility was on my horizon?

I had always told myself to stay positive, even when the worst was happening. This was just another step, another hurdle to overcome. I could get through this.

The steroids they injected into me within the first five days made me very emotional. They were designed to help me regain the use of my right arm, but there was no guarantee. Yet it was my only option. I'd sit, trembling, next to cancer patients in the infusion center, which was a truly humbling experience. I'd get into a reclining chair, and they'd pump me with steroids to help my right arm gain feeling again. I only told my assistant at work about my condition when I called to set up a system for voice technology. I didn't think I could type anymore. I didn't want to be unable to do my job. But I brushed that bit aside when I came in for my first bout of injections.

Staying in the hospital room for the first treatment felt like a punishment. The nurse attending me was kind, sympathetic. She asked me if I wanted to stay in the hospital to receive the remaining steroid treatments. It was at the start of COVID-19 lockdowns, and I just wanted to go home.

Still feeling raw, and to take my mind off my condition, I asked the nurse almost absentmindedly, "How long have you been working here?" She answered with a number I barely registered. I nodded and glanced over at her. My brain scan still hung behind her.

I swallowed, almost afraid to ask the next question. "You must have seen a lot of patients with this diagnosis. How bad is my MRI? How bad does my brain look compared to other people's you've seen?"

Then she looked at me with the kind of power I can still feel. "You know what, Kim? I'll tell you this. Fourteen years ago, when I was diagnosed, my brain looked a lot worse than your picture."

My jaw dropped. Even my upbringing in a German household couldn't prevent me from tearing up. The vision in my head included a wheelchair. I'd imagined reaching a point when I couldn't walk anymore, couldn't use my hands. "But you're working," I stammered. "You're taking my blood pressure."

"Yeah," she said. "I've been a nurse ever since I was diagnosed. You've got this."

She prompted me to stay positive—a concept I'd already adopted years earlier, but one that was invaluable coming from somebody who had already overcome so much. That simple testimony I heard from a nurse when I thought my life was over will forever stick with me. I was shocked to see that she was fully physically functioning with no appearance of disability. It was a sign of hope and something I will never forget.

You never truly know where you're going to end up. You never truly know the path your life will take. Uncertainty is merely a fact of life. The truth is that you'll never know the end of your story. Every step is like that first step into the unknown. Every step is unlike the one before it.

But there's something beautiful about that. There's something unique about the wilds of the unknown. But if you brave it, it'll be an adventure unlike any you've seen before.

2

An Eye on the Horizon

INGE KRIEGER

May 6, 1945, was the first day I took a deep breath in a long time. Though for many, the idea of a fallen Germany was a cause for fear, for me, it meant the war—Hitler's war—was finally over.

American trucks raced through the little town of Dresden, and there was an uncomfortable silence that followed. Germany had surrendered, which meant that it was up for grabs. After the First World War, Dresden plunged into economic hardship, as did the rest of Germany. There was hyperinflation, economic instability, and a significant change in the manufacturing industry. What's more, the vacuum of power left from the First World War had led to a significant change in Germany's future. What would truly happen? We didn't know.

The Yalta agreement had been signed just a few months earlier. What did that mean? To me, it meant the end of everything I knew.

To ensure this would never happen again, Germany was split among the Allies. The Soviets took over everything to the east, while the west was occupied by the Americans, British, and French. The vast difference in ideological and political motivations created a greater rift in the country I had once known. Those in the west were freer to move about, but those in the east …

The Yalta agreement was like a death sentence. The Russian troops advanced. After a time, I saw fewer and fewer American trucks—the trucks that provided aid.

In those days, the rumors ran wild. There were such terrible rumors about the Russian troops, the kind that frightened women and were told in hushed voices like ghost stories. In the early days, my cousin called. She was a refugee fleeing to Dresden with her mother. I tried to convince her to come and stay with us, using the streetcar still in operation. We waited. She didn't come.

It was only later I learned that the night she'd called, Russian soldiers had come and ransacked the apartment houses. The Russians had been looking for women—particularly, beautiful women. In fear, neighbors had pointed up to my uncle's apartment, where they knew my cousin lived. The Russians had found her and had brutally raped her. Anemarie was an organist, very talented and quite sensitive at heart. Her sensitive being couldn't take it, and she had jumped out of the window to her death.

I cried over her passing. Such a loss. I wondered until I was at death's door, if we had just picked her up, could we have saved her?

Attitudes quickly changed as a result of the Communist regime. I noted that friends and family, once so close, suddenly viewed my father as a dirty capitalist. Father hadn't had work since the war's end, but his reputation as a businessman was enough to disgust the neighbors. Even our poverty, stripping the family down to mere rations of food, didn't make us equals.

At that time, a fog of distrust covered Dresden. Whom could we trust? Was everything a lie? It was not enough to tear down the spirit. I looked to the heavens, questioning God—why He would allow the bombing of a beautiful old city, why my brothers and other good German boys had to die, and why the Russians had to destroy such a beautiful place.

It would be some time before I reunited with old friends. Everything seemed slow.

My mother cared for a nice garden full of fruits and vegetables. On one occasion, Russian soldiers came in a big truck to pick our cherry tree, but she blew a whistle and sent the Russian soldiers packing. They never tried again.

Father taught me carpentry. He thought if I could learn the trade, I could take over for him someday and rebuild what had come down in the war. This occupation couldn't last much longer, we reasoned. It had to end soon. Though we learned Russian in school to better understand the Russian soldiers, we all thought it was a temporary measure.

After a time, the Russians settled in army family houses. They stole frequently, and young girls were told to stay home, to not be seen. Vodka flowed freely. Many who had means were quickly targeted, and they were soon just as poor as any other German.

It became a frequent fancy for many to move west.

One day, when I visited a friend in West Germany, I came upon a young man named Fritz. He invited my friend and me to the movies. He took walks with us and served chocolate drinks, a specialty. It seemed such a vast difference from the Communism I had grown to know. Such a luxury. West Germany seemed a dream compared to what I had just left. With such a stark contrast, I became acutely aware of one nightmare traded for another—Hitler's Germany for Stalin's East Germany.

While my family and I struggled just to maintain proper nutrition, Fritz sent me letters. "Make a break from the East," he kept insisting. My father and my mother were the only ones left; my brothers were long gone. Surely, I couldn't leave my family. But soon, unable to hide my desire to escape, I discussed fleeing East Germany with them. Father had addresses in the American zone. My cousin could help me to the border and give me some help. I had no visa to go to the West, only my driver's license and birth certificate. And where would I go? I only had vague ideas.

I packed light. Some clothing and treasured books were all I carried.

My cousin called. She and her husband would help me find a connection to make it into West Germany. The southwest portion was under American control, which was the place I was destined to go.

Looking back is like looking over my shoulder. We had lost a horrible war: We had lost our sons, cousins, brothers. We had moved from one dictatorship to another. Jobs were scarce, and jealousy raised its head toward all those who had a little more. The former enemy was strutting around and living in homes my people had been asked to leave. Yet through it all, Father's roses in the garden were still blooming. The garden continued to produce food. Such a strange clash, such a separation between the light and the dark. I didn't know if I would make it back. I didn't know if my parents would leave such a depressed lifestyle. I didn't know if one of my brothers would eventually come home. No one returned from the monstrous war. They were all taken, gone. There were no graves, and no one was given a funeral. Where was my Heavenly Father? He seemed so far away.

I had to leave in secret. It seemed like my life was nothing but a series of short goodbyes.

The guide taking me to West Germany told me where I had to go and asked for some money as we headed off. He soon left me because Russian soldiers were spotted in the distance. It would mean trouble if we were caught, and my guide didn't want to be part of that. I felt deserted and increased the speed of my steps. I had to slow down. If someone noticed, they would think I was running away.

The next step of my journey, the next town, came into view. I desperately knocked on the door of my contacts, but they turned me away and told me to try a hotel. No one was allowed on the streets after ten at night. I quickly made it to the hotel. They said I could stay if I didn't mind sharing the room. My eyes darted around as I asked her how I could get across the border. She told me about a milk truck and where I could meet the driver and ask him to take me through the posted border patrol.

I slept fitfully until eventually awakening at 2:40 a.m. to meet the milk truck. I stepped out of the shadows at the milkman's residence and asked if there was a chance I could go with them. They didn't care to do it, seeing as they never were paid by anyone, but they still allowed me to lie down between the milk cans. They covered me up with a tarp, and I wasn't to move, cough, or let out a peep. We drove off.

I heard the squeak of the milk truck stopping. Someone shoved a rifle butt into the tarp and hit the milk cans. It must have been the border patrol or Russian soldiers. My heart raced for several moments until they gave the OK to move on.

Sometime later, the milkman dropped me off at a train station and told me to get my ticket quickly and then wait in the restroom until the train came. They didn't want me to get caught, to get sent back.

I boarded the train as quickly as I could without raising suspicions. I sat down in my seat, staring out the window. An American soldier came to inspect my passport. I tried to avoid eye contact with him as I fiddled with my purse. My face grew bright red. Maybe he could see how much I was struggling, how much fear I had. He simply said, "I'll come back for it," but, somehow, I knew he never would.

I heaved a sigh and looked out the window. I was being whisked farther and farther away from Mom and Dad. How were they doing? Were they surviving? Then my thoughts turned to myself. What would life have in store for me? How would God lead me?

He had helped me thus far. Somehow, I knew there was a bright future ahead.

RUNNING FORWARD

Sports were an escape for me.

Maybe it was the way they distracted me from my childhood turmoil, or maybe it was just because I felt like I was following in my family's footsteps. My dad was an athlete in his own right, and my mom was very active. She still is. At seventy-five, she still swims at least five miles each week and bikes the number of miles she turns on her birthday. That spunk, that direct desire to be active, has always inspired me.

I started playing T-ball at an early age, and I was surprisingly good at it. At that age, everyone was all arms and legs, but I guess I turned that to my advantage. The boys noticed my skills and invited me to play baseball with them at recess. They thought I was cool. I could hit the ball just as far, if not farther, than they could.

That athletic streak expanded to include basketball and then volleyball. Throughout my youth, I played sports. When I reached high school, I played three sports. But I always excelled at softball. And that's what got me noticed. I was on the all-star teams. I was the best in my small community, and when you're the best, you get more opportunities. Recruiters asked me to play in college.

It was like a dream. Growing up in difficult circumstances, finding comfort in sports, and then being paid to do what I loved? It became an addiction. I was obsessed. My parents encouraged it as well, proud and thrilled at my decision to play in college.

Augustana University in Sioux Falls, South Dakota, seemed like the best fit for me. It was a private college, prestigiously endowed with the title of Division II National Champions the year I was recruited. It was a remarkable step up. Now I was playing in the big leagues.

I was sure I would fit right in, excel just as I had in my small town, but it didn't really turn out that way.

I found myself playing with some of the best women in the nation. I was no longer unique, no longer special. Instead of carrying games on my shoulders, I was now thrust into a team environment that didn't have nearly the same level of dependence on me. I was just one in a crowd, albeit a crowd extremely skilled and versed in softball.

I stayed in lockstep with the other women on my team. They were all just as committed as I was. We all wanted to be the best in the nation. We were developing as a team, and I was quickly learning the value of becoming a true team member. At a highly competitive level, I saw the irreplaceable value of all my teammates. We were in sync, working like a well-oiled machine. I'd already spent years honing my skills as an individual player, but this was a new experience altogether. It was exciting—riveting—to see myself adapting and changing to accommodate the other women on my team. We became like a family.

Life quickly became a blur. I found myself diving deeply into the world of softball. We needed to maintain the proper physiques—to stay a cut above the rest—to really make it as elite athletes. I needed to be agile, strong, and have that burst of speed when I needed it. That meant hitting the gym daily to hone my technique and improve my game performance. That meant mentally conditioning myself to prepare for games. That meant staying homed in on a diet I knew would work for me. That meant total commitment.

I was still a proficient student. I always had been, and I wasn't going to let that part of myself fade. But it was becoming increasingly difficult to maintain that lifestyle. Games took me away from my classes on a regular basis. Of course, my professors understood.

People involved in sports often missed lectures. And I was hardly the only one doing so.

But there was another problem.

One day, while looking in the mirror, I caught a new side of myself. I was following the ritual I had for the past years: work out, maintain a balanced and nutritious diet, stay fit and athletic. For two years on that scholarship, I had become addicted to working out. Our body fat was tested regularly. We had to weigh in weekly. We had to submit a journal of what we ate. We were national champions. We were in the Women's College World Series. In my freshman year, I had played a ton of games, and I was well on my way to becoming a professional athlete outside of college walls. I wasn't the same Kim I had been when I had left my hometown.

I had made an impact since leaving. I was in the paper weekly and on the local news in high school. In college, I was on national TV. People back home had seen me on ESPN, playing in the Women's College World Series. My hometown knew me and rooted for me. I had created a shell that matched the public image, but underneath, I'd been neglecting my true self.

That desperate attempt to maintain the figure of an athlete had deteriorated my body. Only then did I begin to realize that I had an athletics-induced eating and compulsive exercising disorder. Maybe it was a shock, and maybe it wasn't. I had known that I was committing my entire life to softball, but maybe I hadn't seen the signs?

I suddenly realized that I had spent nearly every entire day working out, practicing, going to classes, and doing homework as a mind-numbing ritual. I was obsessed with remaining athletic while at the same time remaining at the top in academics. I was pushing myself to the extreme, a skill I had practiced for many years, a skill I was proud of, but it was tearing me apart.

I had entered a new life of possibilities. I could actively use my skills in the sporting world to further my academic career as well. But it just wasn't working. I was terribly imbalanced.

So I made a decision—the hardest of my life.

Another college had talked to me about a position on their softball team. It had been on the back burner of my mind when I first attended Augustana University. It was a level below what I was currently playing at, but it was still a reputable school with strong academics. Best of all, it wouldn't require such an intense time commitment athletically. It was a great school, but its athletics ranked in Division III. I likely wouldn't be on ESPN anymore. I wouldn't make the local news as frequently. I would simply play for their softball team without the same athletic time commitment.

But it would give me an escape. I could prioritize my academic success, not miss classes, and hopefully move into a more balanced life.

THE CIRCUMSTANCES THAT CHANGE US

I was a mere twenty years old when I decided to switch universities, but that decision changed my life. I was walking away from an athletic scholarship to focus more on myself and climb out of the rut I'd dug for myself.

It's funny. If you analyze the decisions you made at such a young age, they seem simple. I needed to make that decision to further my career. The move opened the door in my senior year of college to have a more professional focus. Both schools had a prestigious standing, and both of them could have opened the door to impressive professional successes. However, I needed to make a shift that simply wasn't possible at my first university. I needed to focus on a balance for myself—to get healthy, to change who I was into someone I could maintain. And I went through a transformation I hadn't expected.

Our circumstances put us on paths we need to be on, and, sometimes, those paths lead to the most difficult decisions. Those transitions are painful yet poignant.

So many of us go through similar transitions. The paths we go down may seem automatic after a while. We tell ourselves we've been put on this track, and it's too much bother to get off this train. Soon, circumstances may become harder and harder. It's more difficult to maintain the same level of motivation you once had. It may even feel, at some points, that breathing the same air is more difficult than it was before.

It's often at these points that we lose faith in what we are supposed to do. Maybe we once had a vision that we believe is now lost. But is it really?

I needed to go through the struggles of burnout to realize I needed to make a serious transformation. I realized I wasn't being true to myself anymore. The shift midway through my college career may have seemed outright crazy to many people. I had been making headway in both sports and academics. I had been on the path to rocketing success. In fact, later, I was even inducted, along with my teammates, into the Augustana College Hall of Fame. I had been going places. So why did I stop?

I'd come to a crossroads in my mental attitude. I was riding that same train, following that same line. *You just need to push through it*, I thought. But that pivotal moment in my life came because of a close look in the mirror. The person looking back at me didn't represent what I wanted to see.

When I saw that image, the solution became easy. The truth is that difficult decisions are often easy solutions. It takes a gut-wrenching acknowledgment to realize you're not who you want to be, and that's where the pain surfaces. It's hard to look in the mirror and realize you're not being true to yourself. When you are chasing a dream you thought you wanted, it's excruciating to realize it's not where you're meant to be.

But overcoming that schism in your soul starts with a simple statement: "Everything is going to be OK."

Developing a positive mindset is the key to differentiating the harmful from the positive. Those terrifying moments of uncertainty that keep us from experiencing the possibilities are the guards blocking us from a fruitful life. It takes a strong PMA to realize that those axe-wielding guards are nothing but vapors of smoke.

IMPLANTING THE HEART OF A NATION

I was never more aware of my inclination to open my heart than when I went to India.

I went there on business initially. I was there to make connections, hand out business cards, and connect my culture with that of the people there. But when I stepped off the airplane and made it further into Indian territory, I was speechless.

When I stepped into a more corporate landscape, I suddenly felt extremely aware of myself: what I was wearing, what my body language was saying, how I was presenting myself. In India, women were expected to wear skirts below the knee. I needed closed-toe shoes that were neatly maintained. I needed subtle makeup and a respectful hairstyle. It was similar to the way that I would dress back home, with much more attention to modesty.

When I talked to fellow professionals, I maintained my natural friendliness and openness. That's what they expected, and I was only too happy to oblige. We were similar, engaging in the same type of work, but we were worlds apart.

The cultural dissonance was astonishing. There was an extremely stark difference between the wealthy and the poor. I'd never seen such poverty. Small homes were stacked upon each other, filled to the brim with people. Streets were abuzz with the sounds of people selling products and the heavy footfalls of everyone traversing the marketplace. I could look down and see children running back and forth, some of them barely conscious of me, while others held out their hands, begging for money. Their fingers seemed so small, their eyes pleading. It's something I'd never anticipated before making my trip. I had been so naive. I hadn't realized just how different our cultures were, even though one might expect that.

I hadn't realized the extent of the poverty outside the United States. The people in India were surviving on so little. What's more, they were actually smiling.

It got me thinking: Am I grateful for the things that I have? Do I bow my head in reverence to the people who came before me? Do I take for granted the things that were given to me?

For a long time, I expected a lot of myself. I worked for everything I had. I fought very hard for it. But there was something about seeing those tiny fingers of the lower-caste street children reaching up to me, desperately asking for something I could give them, that truly made me pause.

Up until that point, I had worked in the corporate world for at least a decade. I had already had two children by that point. My hectic schedule made me feel like I was never around, living life in a blur. But the trip to India really made me stop and think. I was truly grateful for all I had, but was there something else in my life I wanted? Something I was depriving myself of just for the sake of staying busy at my job?

I received something of a spiritual awakening during those few days in India. Walking in the streets made me realize that I was missing something in my personal life. I'd wanted another child, but there never seemed to be enough time. But did I really want to reach the age of seventy and regret not having another child?

After the whirlwind of my few days in India, I'd made up my mind. It was vitally important to me to have another child if I was able. The fear I'd felt was just a hindrance on my journey. I knew what I had to do. There was much more to be gained by listening to my heart.

Since that day, I've been back to India many times. The country holds a special place in my heart. It's the place that reminds me of my need for gratitude. It's the place that makes me realize my life can be so much more than any box I put myself into.

TAKING THE BAD WITH THE GOOD

Have you ever looked at yourself in the mirror and wondered when this trial will end. Maybe you've become bogged down with the never-ending struggle you've been feeling. Perhaps the seemingly never-ending drudgery of showing up to a job you hate makes you want to scream. Maybe you've found yourself putting your hands over your ears in a frustrating attempt to drown out an argument you've heard for the thousandth time. Perhaps the decisions of another have painted you into a corner you can't seem to escape. Have you looked into the mirror and not recognized the person staring back at you? At times like those, it's difficult to take a step back and realize that things will work out eventually.

To those who know me, it's unsurprising that I'm a fan of simply putting my head down and focusing on the task. I'm a masterful triple-tasker who's execution-focused and determined to achieve near perfection if possible. But there's value in just completing the work, even if you don't know what's going to happen. And the hard, difficult times will always come. You can't control every aspect of your life, try as you might. Some things happen despite every possible effort to prevent problems from occurring. It's a simple, if annoying, fact of life.

But hang in there.

Most of us go through trials for a reason. Maybe it's to strengthen our resolve to achieve what we want. Or it may be to find the inspiration we need to change tactics. Whatever your direction is, you won't find the solution if you give up.

Understanding Your Direction

I think we'd all like to believe that the answers to life's questions can be found in a book, on a phone, or from a loved one. Others have gone through similar adversities before, which means that there must be a reasonable explanation at our fingertips, right?

It's a shame that today, far too few of us trust our guts. Far too few of us actually know ourselves. Far too few of us spend time asking the questions only our guts can answer. There are some questions we can only ask and some decisions we can only make if we know who we are.

My grandmother's experiences primed her for a life-changing event, one that wouldn't have occurred if she'd just stayed where she was. It was a dangerous mission, but a need for escape guided her. For others, the choice to leave wouldn't have been the right one.

But it was for her.

It was worth the risk to see a beautiful future on the other side. Often, it's worth the risk to choose a difficult lifestyle in the pursuit of happiness, and she knew she had so much more waiting for her on the other side.

Understanding the possibilities for your future comes down to knowing who you truly are. If you're unhappy with where you are, constantly stressed, and constantly feeling as though there is some imbalance in your life, you're not going in the right direction. Your path in life can't be determined by someone else. The inspiration you have for the life you want is merely one path among an infinite number. You're your own hero. With the right push, you could be greater than you ever thought you could be.

Experiencing the Heartache

But I don't want to paint a picture that is too rosy. Merely being unhappy with your circumstances now doesn't indicate that you're doing the wrong thing. No one gets through life without experiencing some challenges.

What about those times you had to say goodbye to loved ones in your life? Maybe someone you loved passed away. Maybe you broke up with someone you were deeply in love with. Maybe you felt the pain of heartache through someone else's experience. Whatever the case, those difficult moments of pain always come.

But if you could take away that pain, would you?

Those moments of deep pain and anguish teach us something about ourselves we couldn't have learned anywhere else.

As I walked the streets of India, I experienced something I never had before. That level of poverty didn't seem possible to me. I had grown up poor myself, so for the longest time, I had believed that I had known hardship and come out the other side. Yet my experience in India only taught me how little I truly knew. I saw hopeless children on the street with missing fingers and with no shoes. I saw so many people surviving on so little.

Those moments when my heart broke for someone else gave me the perspective I needed to live my life a little better.

We go through our lives trying to avoid the negatives. That's not to say we don't focus on them, merely that we wish to evade some of life's most difficult circumstances. But that sort of lifestyle is miserable to maintain. How could we appreciate the sunshine without the rain? How could we delight in the good times without ever knowing the bad?

So, instead of merely remaining oblivious to the negatives—a coping strategy that is ultimately detrimental to your soul—face them with a PMA. Those heartaches are there for a reason. Those moments of pain teach us something. But it's only possible to see through the haze of disappointment by shining the light of positivity on what could be.

Fleeing from Fear

I often tell people that the most difficult decision in my life happened when I was twenty. The change in universities came with an astronomical shift in my view of life. Looking back now, I can't imagine making a different decision. The journey that decision took me on was precisely what I needed to grow. It was my period of transformation, something I never would have experienced had I listened to my fear.

We often miss opportunities to grow because we're afraid to take that next step. Justifying a change of pace, a change of scenery, a change of circumstances, is frightening. And, if you let it, that fear can obstruct your path forward.

I have often found that the things most worth doing are the things that have frightened me the most.

I can't count the times I believed I had too little time, too little resources, or too little knowledge. Sometimes, it felt like I was standing on a ledge, unsure if I could ever truly know what would happen if I stepped forward.

I think most of us have gone through this countless times in our lives, if not daily.

But what if you take a step back from that ledge for a moment? The truth is that fear and positivity can't exist in the same place. If you're truly unsure about the future, if you let your fears take over, positivity can't come through. So take a deep breath, step back, and let yourself imagine the possibilities for a moment. Your future is bright. Don't let the fog of doubt and fear shroud that beautiful view.

A STEP INTO THE FUTURE

Of course, sometimes that fear is the starting point to propel you to something greater.

I met my husband in circumstances rather familiar to many people. I graduated from university in May 1996 after four years and started a computer engineering job two months later. It was a bit of a leap from my business administration major to information technology (IT), but I knew that life skill was important, and I was eager to learn more.

Those first few years were a whirlwind.

I was still fascinated by the possibilities before me. My mother had gotten a degree, of course, but this was still new territory for most of my family. My sister had gone back to graduate school, and I knew I had to do the same, even if from nothing more than a sense of pride. Perhaps it was an innate desire to be like her that drew me to graduate school. The problem was that I needed to work for two years before I went back for my master's degree. They want you to get more experience, to get the practical application, before you start. So, it was decided for me: I would work full-time for two years before going back for my MBA.

I aimed to get my MBA quickly. I didn't want to spend too much time in classes when I could be getting ahead in my career. Working full-time and taking classes, I could get it done in four years. It would be a huge feat, but it was possible. And I was all about finding the possible.

Unfortunately, like many things in life, it didn't work out exactly as I had planned it.

During the third year of my MBA program, I got pregnant with my first child, who was born in January 2001. It was definitely a blessing, but it did come with its own set of challenges because of my shift in priorities. A work–life balance? What a dream. I got up nightly for six months so my baby could eat. I took night classes and pumped milk in a bathroom stall at college. At the same time, I continued to work full-time.

I found myself falling into a well of duty. Looking back now, I don't really know how I did it. When you're a mother, it's like you have superpowers. Remarkably, I didn't need as much sleep then. At that point, I guess my body just figured I would make it up later in life. I was a full-time mother and employee, and a part-time student. But I did what I had to do.

What should have taken me another six months to complete eventually became an additional year. But the results were amazing. During the time I studied for my MBA, I worked with people from all over the world, many of whom were from the Asia-Pacific region. It was a time when I felt like I was drifting with the tide, taking advantage of the opportunities I had and the decisions I had made. I was growing at an alarming rate.

It was at this time that I started unintentionally climbing the corporate ladder. Getting a graduate degree broadened my horizons. Looking back, though, I hadn't needed the MBA to get where I am today. I had just needed to scratch that itch, to learn more. But I found that the more I challenged myself, the more I grew.

I can't believe the life I've lived. I can't believe I made it through. But I wouldn't change it for anything.

I don't think of the difficulties I endured as setbacks or failures. There were opportunities for growth and learning that I never would have gotten if I hadn't lived through those sleep-deprived days. I look back now, and I smile.

I'm sure you can look back at many times in your life and wonder how you did it—that weight that you felt crushing you at the time was somehow bearable. Despite not taking your eyes off the road in front of you, you were making progress, even if it was just an inch at a time.

I wonder if I could do the same thing now. I believe myself to be very strong-willed, so could I force myself to do it now?

The reality is that I'm sure I can take whatever life hands me. But it's not the tons of weight on my back that I'll be counting. I'll keep my eyes fixed on the horizon—that place where all the possibilities lie, the place where I'm destined to end up.

3

Aspiring to Greatness

INGE IBS, NÉE KRIEGER

The train lulled me to sleep.

The feeling of freedom, an escape from persecution, had rushed over me. Years later, I wouldn't remember much of that train ride. The fear had left me.

I finally exited the train in the depot of Garmisch-Partenkirchen. There was a dampness still in the air, one that felt like an embrace. Fritz worked at the building office and had to wait for the last train before he could close up shop. But there I was. There he was. We were glad to see each other, yet it felt kind of strange. There was a border between my parents and my friends, my original family and my new family.

Fritz took me to a rented apartment to live with a Bavarian family. The owner of the home, Mrs. Hetzer, was very kind, and she had also come from behind the Iron Curtain. The whole family had. The rooms were cozy and welcoming. The setup of the house was different from the one I had come to know, but this whole adventure was new.

Back home, the drudgery continued. A quick call home informed me that refugees were now living with my family. Business was slow for Dad.

But I had found a second home here. I had acquired a carpenter's job in town, incredibly, living off the skills my father had taught me when I was young. I'd made friends too. I met Brigitte; she roomed upstairs. We shared food and stories, helping each other whenever we could. She photographed farms and families after World War II. Because money was scarce, her clients often paid with food. She still made a living as a photographer, and, occasionally, she would leave her daughter with me when she went to work.

Brigitte would tell me miraculous stories as we sat in my two-bedroom apartment. We comforted each other. We celebrated our first Christmas together with a goose. We shared that Christmas dinner with everyone in our house: Fritz, Brigitte, her daughter, and the Kuntze family, another family living upstairs. It felt good to smile during Christmas again. We joked about how to cook the meat, laughed at past events, and enjoyed each other's company.

Back home, my parents didn't eat well that day.

But on the other side of the Iron Curtain, my joy was just beginning. Fritz and I continued to spend time together, existing in a bubble, a secluded haven from where I had originally come. He told me of the possibility of moving to America. Fritz had been born in Chicago, an American citizen by birth, but was raised in Germany. That itself was a struggle. The Americans didn't want to recognize him as a citizen. The Germans didn't want him to lose his German citizenship. Ultimately, he had to choose one or the other. Because Germany was so divided, even though it had been his home for most of his life, he chose his American citizenship.

The stark changes in my recent life yielded another surprise: I was pregnant. Of course, that meant I would go with him. I had made my decision the day I set foot on that milk truck. I had chosen Fritz over everyone else. It was bold to consider that I would leave my home. But perhaps that was just another step in God's journey for me. Suddenly, a decision that had once seemed so frightening now seemed exciting. A few months later, I gave birth to my precious son, Fritz Jr.

We waited until my parents could join us for our marriage ceremony. We were able to arrange their arrival by train. The reunion was tearful but ecstatic. For my parents, it was almost as though they had a son again.

Arrangements were made for the wedding, and all that remained was our appointment at the courthouse at nine in the morning to sign our marriage license. As it happened, producing Fritz's birth certificate to sign our marriage certificate lit a fire, and his citizenship was recognized. Finally, we could move to the United States. It was a marvelous surprise, something of a wedding present.

Walking down that aisle, surrounded by the people who loved Fritz and me, is among the most beautiful experiences in my life. I was adorned in a beautiful maroon silk dress. My father walked me down the aisle. Yet, doubt seeped in. I realized during that fateful walk that if I said yes, I would be agreeing to move to the US. Was I really ready for that? I'd always felt responsible for my parents. They had gone through so much, lost their two beautiful sons, and now they would lose me as well, if only for a time. America seemed so far away. But perhaps the question was instead, could I leave little Fritz without a father?

At times, life seems to pull us in all directions. The people I loved seemed to have a hold on me, and I felt as though I was needed everywhere. My parents struggled terribly in East Germany. My new child needed a strong mother. Fritz needed me. But, as I looked up at him while walking down the aisle, the decision was already made in my heart. I walked down the aisle and said yes to my new husband and my new life.

That night, I raised a glass to toast my new marriage and my new life.

A TRANSFORMATION PERSPECTIVE

Living exceptionally comes down to an inner desire to adapt and move on. Are we willing to let a chaotic life help us shift to a new adventure, or do we choose to sink?

I believe there's a great advantage in setting ambitious goals and keeping tabs on where you are. Like my grandmother before me, I see the vast importance of making decisions that aren't easy but are necessary for personal growth.

But that wasn't always the case. It took a great deal of time to convince myself that I wasn't on the path I thought I should be on.

Sometime in the middle of a tenure working at Target, I took part in a survey in a small group setting regarding the direct reports of my team. They had all filled out a survey on their leader—me. All the categories boasted positive reviews. I excelled in collaboration, execution, and critical thinking. All the categories were glowing, except one. I hadn't yielded a high result on the "get to know you" section.

The results came as a bit of a shock. My signature personality was still one of extroversion. I have always loved being around people, and I particularly delight in building good relationships with the people I work with. The people who work for me, my coworkers, my supervisors, everybody. I felt as though I was the most open-book person in the group.

Suddenly feeling disconcerted, I proactively asked my team about it. Darren Matthews raised his hand—a courageous move and one I still look on with pride—and said, "Kim, we don't really know you. You're kind of like a robot. You get in before everybody and stay longer than everybody else. You don't forget anything. You just work hard. So, we don't know the real you."

Probably like most people working to get ahead in their careers, I had set work in a separate section of my life. It's not like I'm the first person to claim a work–life balance, holding onto the belief that what is at work stays at work and what is at home stays at home. At work, I had a different role to fill. And that's not to mention the singularity of my situation. I was among the few women in senior leadership positions within the IT department, and a certain emotional detachment seemed only necessary to accommodate my responsibilities. I felt a kind of responsibility to my coworkers to maintain that stoicism to keep my focus. Coincidentally, it wasn't something that I had consciously done. It was just an organizational tendency to keep things in order.

At the same time, I felt an internal duty to exceed the performance of my male counterparts. I was a minority in the IT space. Not to mention, many of my peers didn't talk about their families while I juggled a heavy dual-career household with young children. Something inside me pushed me to follow those robotic tendencies to push through. I felt somewhat isolated—though that feeling might have been only on my side.

I became acutely aware that I wasn't on the path I should be on. I had come back from India with a brand-new lease on life. I knew from my experiences in that country that I wanted to balance myself on a personal scale, but somehow, that hadn't translated to my work.

Where were my priorities? Was I too focused on doing well at the job I already had, or was it my goal to expand, to think bigger? Maybe my priorities weren't simply to maintain. Maybe they were to grow.

So, I expanded my reach. There were always new assignments in big companies. There were always opportunities to grow.

I knew the ins and outs of the managerial side of IT, but there was so much more to it. When I was lucky enough to be hired at my first company in July 1996, they trained me as a computer engineer. I went through a six-month crash course in computer science and had a mentor to help me prepare for an independent role. At a high level, IT is derived from three functions: planning, building, and running. Many people stay within one of those three domains. As an executive at Target, I'd acquired a fair knowledge of the planning and running portions of IT, but I could do better. Knowing my own tenacity, I knew I could add the building phase to my list of skills.

My path to expansion included far more people. At every step of the way, I was increasingly conscious that I had more to learn. I had already worked in the field for more than ten years, but I hardly knew everything. Though fear was my first instinct, I became determined to open up more about my own vulnerabilities. Miraculously, the holes in my abilities were filled by the caring, nurturing patience of mentors and colleagues.

My path wouldn't have been possible without the benevolence of people who knew far more than I did. I had already determined to become much more open and much more vocal with the people around me, but my work with so many other people cemented that resolve.

Remarkably, the positivity I'd always sought to instill in my personal and professional lives made it possible to become more open and transparent. The life-changing experiences I had came as a result of my insistence to remain positive. With a more peaceful mind, my priorities evened out significantly. And far from losing my focus on my career, I became much steadier, more content than I had been in a long time.

A PUSH FOR EXCELLENCE

My primary goal in life is to be happy, plain and simple. I live in the moment, striving daily to be the best version of myself. Darren Matthews's words had lit a fire in me. I had been far too concerned with making sure that everything followed a plan that I had forgotten the importance of growing.

Of course, that's the problem with most of the stuck points in our lives. The fear of losing it all often prevents us from jumping in. As I have done multiple times in my life, I'm sure we all frequently ask ourselves if we can do it. Sometimes, we believe we are just hanging on, not even moving the needle, merely preventing it from dropping down a degree. But other times, that frustratingly desperate desire to stay the same for fear of losing everything is exactly what keeps you standing still while the world continues to turn.

Each of us struggles along an ever-shifting path. Sometimes, that path is easy, downhill. Sometimes, that path takes unexpected turns. And at other times—though this might seem like the most common phase—the path skyrockets at a steep upward incline. The fears we accumulate from childhood are inevitably shackled to our ankles as we shift along the path. During the downward portions, sometimes, it seems as if they are not there at all. But on the upward climbs, they make it seem as though we're constantly slipping.

But what if, instead of struggling to maintain our footholds upward on the path of life, we simply let go?

Freed from the burdens of crushing fears, we can start to accomplish anything. The fears that have followed us for as long as we've let them no longer control us. After that, we have no limit, no end to the possibilities of growth.

When we stop thinking of life as a series of things that might hold us back or are too difficult to overcome, it becomes easy to realize there's a way through it all. Any question has an answer. Any hurdle is possible to overcome. Any ambitious goal becomes manageable.

In the grand scheme of things, life is short. You only live once, so it's best to make the most of it. It's impossible to know which opportunities will come and go at different points in life. Take advantage of all life has to offer, and remember that some chances don't come twice.

If, along our journey, life presents stumbling blocks, even roadblocks, it's not an indication to give up. There are points in all our lives where the small things seem to send us over the edge. That small outcropping on the upward trajectory of our lives may seem like an impassable boulder to knock us down. But what if, instead of staying down after a hard fall, we merely stood up, wiped the dust off our clothes, and continued to press forward?

There will always be reasons to say no. There will always be reasons to stop pressing forward and to give up. But are those small inconveniences—large though they may seem to us—really worth a deviation from our path onward?

I've found that the small inconveniences will always be there. There will never be enough time in the day, enough fuel in the tank, or completely clear mental faculties to complete my grand scheme for life. But what does it matter? It's time to let go of the small inconveniences and focus on growth.

It's a cliché to say yes to everything, but maybe it's overstated for a reason. So few of us really take a chance. It's time to say yes to everything—every trip, every new experience. Let nothing slip away.

The bumps and bruises we get from life will always come. Beaten and battered, none of us will escape unscathed. But those scars we receive along the way hardly define us. They're merely a testament to our perseverance.

A PHYSICAL BALANCE

My body had felt the effects of those bruises early on, but they caught up with me again after my tenure at Target.

I hadn't given up physical activity after my college days. I needed the physical pillar in my life to keep myself balanced. So, in my free time, I started to spend a lot of time running. It was a way to keep myself motivated while maintaining my sanity. I was doing so many things, and running was my escape. Getting lost on a trail was a way to drop my focus on my never-ending to-do list.

But I felt myself getting obsessed again.

Sometimes, I would run as many as forty miles a week, consistently running five days a week. It wasn't unusual for me to run more than eight miles a day, and sometimes, I ran even more. To serious runners, running for an hour and a half to two hours a day might not seem like much, but I could feel it taking a toll on my body. At the end of those particularly brutal weeks, I started feeling pain in my hips. That didn't stop me from hitting the trails the next week. I needed that runner's high to get through the week.

When I was running, I felt unstoppable. I ran as an escape, but it became a compulsion. Running was a terrific way to blow off some steam, but when I became obsessed, it harkened back to my twenties.

In those days, I still thought about the pillars holding up my priority balls. I still thought about the ways I could balance my job, my relationships, my community, and my personal, physical, and mental growth. But it was almost like a part of me couldn't let this go. I knew there was something wrong. I knew I was out of balance. But what else was I going to do? I simply put my head down and kept running.

It was something of a fluke when my sister-in-law came to visit from Nevada and insisted that we go to a yoga class to get a little exercise the morning of Thanksgiving Day. She was looking for something, for a meaningful way to start the holiday, and asked me to join her.

I felt completely out of my element the first day on my mat. I listened intently to the positions called out by the instructor and tried to follow along, but I found myself continually glancing at other students to get a better idea of what to do. I'm no stranger to trying different physical exercises, but this new style was completely new to me. When I exited the building after the lesson, my head was still whirling. But it was exhilarating.

I found a sense of balance on that day that I hadn't felt before. Yoga was a deep connection between physical activity and mental stimulation. It was exactly what I needed. I was hooked.

I stopped running. It's not something I would have expected. I had spent so many years using it to get me through the week, but there was something so peaceful about yoga. Instead of going running every day, I replaced it with going to yoga at that same studio my sister-in-law had taken me to. I started in November 2017, and I haven't stopped going consistently ever since.

That yoga studio became the headquarters of my mental and physical growth. I wasn't satisfied with simply remaining a student. I always felt like there was something more to learn, something more to give. I went through 250 hours to become a certified instructor, and in 2022, I became a teacher there. I focus on positivity, bringing peace to people who attend my classes. It is a way for me to stay mentally balanced, but more than that, it is a way for me to help other people stay positive and grounded as well. All of us grow in that studio, both physically and mentally.

THE ART OF LETTING GO

When most people think of success, they attribute it to pushing harder, putting in long hours, and exhausting themselves to get ahead. Remarkably, I've found that it's quite often more important to let go.

Letting go of your ego allows others to come in and fill in the gaps in your life. Letting go of small inconveniences frees up your mind to focus on the really important things. Letting go of your fears encourages you to overcome any obstacle.

In short, letting go lifts you enough to pursue ambitious goals without fear of what will weigh you down.

But the process is curious. When was the last time you gave yourself enough runway to let go? Most of the time, it takes a concerted effort to truly give ourselves a break. All the people on the internet yelling the single accord, "Just let go!" don't understand the quietness and self-reflection required to do just that. To start, all it takes are a few steps.

Mapping Priorities

At any time in your life, leveling your priorities is extremely difficult. The phrase we often hear, "You need to push harder," sometimes only spoken to ourselves, is what gets us out of whack. We strive for greatness by seeking results from one of our priorities instead of creating a balance among them.

I tend to think of life in terms of juggling balls. Each ball represents one of my priorities. For most of us, and probably for most of our lives, we juggle those balls in an unending circle. That creates a disparity in the importance of each ball at different parts of our lives. It became clear when I reevaluated how I communicated with the people I worked with that I wasn't approaching things in a way that would level each of my balls. It was time to change things.

At multiple times in my life, I realized I couldn't keep going at the pace I had been. I was too focused on succumbing to my surroundings and doing the best I could. Many times, my career was my highest priority, and it was time that I leveled the balls again. That meant I needed to lower the priority on my career ball in favor of the others.

I didn't care what that meant for my job title. I needed to make the time for laughter, family, friends, the little things.

When I feel that one priority is taking precedence over the others, I take a step back and reevaluate.

Developing a Road Map

Once I have a plan of success for my priorities, I can incorporate those ideas into a future road map. To stay on track, it's not just about the quantitative metrics that I take. I also evaluate how I'm feeling, the feedback from people around me, and my personal reflections. The small problems, the small inconveniences that get in the way, are easier to overcome if I have evidence of past success.

For me, having a visual aid gives me a better idea of how well I'm succeeding. I have a notebook, always kept under my computer monitor, that contains the activities I want to experience. There are constant reminders for me to stay on the right path. Remarkably, sometimes, even just the feel of my notebook, always knowing that it's with me, gives me the confidence to ensure I live life to the fullest and do not settle.

But perhaps the greatest gauge is my personal happiness. Is what I'm doing truly preparing me to become the best person I could possibly be? Are the people around me happy? Am I unbalanced in my priorities, or am I giving it all to everything I want to do?

I'm developing my life in pursuit of others, but it's just as important to me that I am fulfilled and healthy. I can't continue to give of myself if I have no more fuel in the tank.

Taking It Slow

What good is the struggle if you can't maintain a happy demeanor?

A few years ago, I tore my anterior cruciate ligament taking a wrong turn on a black diamond ski hill. I caught a patch of ice and went down hard, hearing a distinct pop in my knee. It seemed bad, but I got up and kept skiing. Nearly two weeks later, while playing hockey, I had to admit to myself there was a problem. The decision before me was surgery or no surgery. Because I have MS and knew the consequences might include losing the use of my legs, weighing the timing of this surgery was more complicated. I didn't know if I'd still be able to walk in two years, and the thought of a one-year recovery seemed to take precious time I just wasn't sure I should sacrifice.

The times you fall flat on your face while reaching for the stars are among the most frustrating. We all want success. We all want to grow. The speed bumps we encounter along the way can throw a wrench in our progression if we're not careful. Like my own struggles with MS, the diagnosis of an illness, and the long recovery from an injury, the detrimental effect of lost memories are all parts of life at some point. The path to success is littered with people who didn't get up when they tripped over a particularly nasty obstacle.

Everyone can recover from these detrimental experiences. Life isn't exactly known for its pleasant paths, and everyone must spend at least part of their lives picking themselves up from particularly hard falls. But the people who ultimately continue to press forward are the people who put a smile on their faces, even when they don't feel like it.

One of life's greatest mysteries is the path we're going to take. I'm sure everyone, at some point in their lives, has looked back and thought, *When I was young, I never thought I would be where I am now.* Instead of fighting against those changes, embrace them. We never know where we are supposed to go when we're looking forward toward our own plans. The paths we take may not be the ones we initially wanted, but maybe they're exactly what we need.

So, instead of rushing forward, dusting ourselves off when we fall, and charging once again, perhaps the best plan is merely to stop, breathe, and smell the roses along the way. We are constantly evolving. The fears we feel today may not be there tomorrow. And grace needs to follow our paths. We'll always get there, even if it's not when we anticipated.

THE CORRECT PILLAR ASSORTMENT

After Darren Matthews's daring pronouncement, I started to take stock of other things in my life.

For the first time ever, I realized the importance of parental transparency. I had hidden my third pregnancy at work until I was almost six months along so that my superiors wouldn't treat me differently. I'd had so much heaped on me that my workload transferred to four people when I finally went on my ten-week leave with my third child. Obviously, I had been overloaded.

Finally, it was time to be more transparent about how draining the whole experience had become. It was time to focus less on how much I could achieve at work and focus more on the community, more on the women who were also struggling in tech, more on my family. In essence, it was time to spend more time balancing my "career ball" and "mom ball" in the air.

I was becoming happier at work, fulfilling what I strongly felt was my purpose to connect with people while simultaneously growing myself.

But that was only the tip of the iceberg.

As my focus on work lowered, I needed to bring up my other priorities. I began to think of the balancing act as establishing pillars for my balls to rest on. One of my balls that needed serious dusting off was my community priority ball.

I'd always wanted to be more community-conscious, but I never seemed to have the time. It was something that I had neglected for years, though it had always been at the back of my mind. I knew I could inspire people around me to take better care of their own communities. It was time to pick up the ball and place it evenly on my set of pillars.

Of course, balancing my priorities came with a lot more work. But, for the first time in a long time, I was a lot more excited to do those things I'd always wanted to do. I realized I was allowing myself to be more creative, to make more interesting choices, and to take better control of my life.

One of my first steps was influencing other women in technology. I chaired a board dedicated to fostering awareness and building a stronger sense of community among women in the field. I also served on a board that worked to introduce inner-city kids to tech career opportunities—something I felt could truly transform their futures. Whether through volunteering, attending fundraisers, or helping with larger campaigns, I've always worked hard to support efforts that really resonated with me. What started as a desire to give back became a defining passion.

My increased attention to the community created a following and started to influence people. I found myself influencing people from around the world, leading them to a better place. It started small. There were times when I would speak to only ten people or to one hundred people. I would start off with a speech or discussion to highlight what women faced in the technology space. But the feeling of helping others was just so monumental to me, so inspiring. I almost felt a high from helping people. My story was important to me, but I hardly realized its impact on others.

My yoga practice had put me in front of people in ways I'd never expected. Occasionally, someone would come up to me after class and thank me for my authenticity. The mental clarity I achieved by sharing ideas was deeply rooted in my soul, and everything I expressed was deeply intentional. I had created these diversions of focus as a way to help myself, but I was slowly realizing that they made a big impact on others too.

I've seen others who hit that stride turn into people in crisis mode. There's just too much attention, too much coming from all angles. Yet, the act of simply putting my life in balance—focusing on community, family, work, and myself—was creating a calm I had never known was missing. The extra workload suddenly seemed doable. I was excited again. I was creating a lifestyle I could live comfortably, almost blissfully.

I was doing more for myself and other people than ever before. Better yet, I was achieving a much higher goal: living a purposeful life. There it was again: the mention of a purposeful life. It seemed that, wherever I went, it was a recurring theme. And it followed me year after year.

The year 2024 marked my fiftieth year. Despite everything, it was a year I'd looked forward to for quite some time. And it marked a time in my life when I began to really concentrate on my potential and progression.

I had set aside a special notebook just for this occasion. I keep it next to me, filled with a list of things I want to do. The little red notebook is tattered by now because of how often I look at it, and it's traveled around the globe with me. It reminds me of all the things I've yet to accomplish.

Just recently, my niece reached out to me. I like to stay in touch with family, and we keep tabs on each other. During our conversation, she brought up the little red notebook. "Have you crossed off a lot of things on your list so far?"

Smiling, I looked down at the red notebook and opened it up to glance at its familiar pages. "No," I said. "I've only crossed a few things off, but that's not really the point. It's important to reach for those ambitious goals, but the most important thing is that pursuing them brings me a sense of purpose and joy."

4

Mental Transformations

INGE IBS

Parting is a drain on the soul.

We'd had so many beautiful reunions, so many connections that had been years in the making, only to have them slip away once again.

Looking back on my wedding day, we had so many blessings. Our friends and family had come so far to see us. Many of them had come from the Communist zone. Fritz had scrambled to find his birth certificate, the one he needed to prove he was an American and an integral part of our marriage certification, which Father Ibs produced. It was a mercy that the search only delayed our wedding for one hour. Did all these events have any significant meaning? They were convenient, true, but they were also much more than that. To me, they were the hand of God.

A painful separation rocked our world early on. Not quite two and a half months after our wedding, Fritz's paperwork was completed. He would go ahead of our son and me to the United States on October 1. We made plans and packed, planning that our son and I would follow him soon. It was a bitter goodbye, but we trusted we'd be together again soon.

I looked toward the mountains that shone with the brilliant colors of the morning sun during those September and October days. It was all coming to an end, and maybe too quickly. A place stricken with such grief, such sorrow, had molded me, and though it was exciting to envision the future in the United States, it still hurt my soul.

But the future looked bright. Fritz would take care of me, and our young son would grow up in the United States. Counting on that blessing, I made boat reservations on the Holland America Line. On the other side of the ocean, Fritz had already gathered furniture and rented an apartment. Frightening as it was, my future was slowly becoming a reality.

November came with grating anxiety. I went to the Munich consulate to receive my first passport to go to the United States. I sat nervously in the consul's office as he drilled me with questions about my upbringing. I was treated like a prisoner in my own country, a slave created by a man who claimed to work for a better life for Germans but only stifled any chance we had to escape. The consul asked that I sign the "green book." After waiting with bated breath, I received an answer I didn't expect:

I wouldn't be receiving my passport that day. My records showed that I had once been in the Jungmädel—the "Young Girls" of the Hitler Youth. Because of the new laws in Allied-occupied Germany, my passport would be withheld for a time.

A pit in my stomach formed as I walked back home, back to the apartment that we weren't supposed to occupy in the future. But now, there was uncertainty.

With a trembling voice, I called to cancel my boat reservations. With tears in my eyes, I let Fritz know we might not be joining him after all. I could imagine the smile leaving his face as he told me he would cancel the apartment. He would give it all up. We could never really know when I could follow him to the United States.

It seemed like a sick nightmare. This long journey, this exceeding hardship, but for what? It seemed like we had come so far only to be stopped in our tracks.

But one word kept coming to mind: patience.

Letters flowed back and forth between Wisconsin and Bavaria. An old friend of Fritz's came to visit me often. She, too, was leaving for the United States to be with her husband. But, because of the new law, she was stranded on Ellis Island. It had taken one week for her husband to get her out, and he was stationed at Fort Campbell, Kentucky, in the army. He had a better shot than most. But, as often seems to happen, things worked out.

While my heart was overseas with Fritz, I was feeling the familiar tug from East Germany. My mom and dad struggled to keep the buildings they owned. The Kommandatura had already hauled my father in twice for questioning. The strikes had become so bad that friends had told him to leave. "Take the train to Berlin and stay with friends," they pleaded. It all sounded so easy. Leaving a hellscape for freedom, a chance to start a new life. But it came at the cost of the old life. Everything they had built together, they would have to leave behind. Was it worth the chance?

To my father, it was. There was only so much my parents could take. Kissing my mother goodbye, my father boarded the train and headed into the Allied-occupied zone. Hunkered down in a cart filled with others like him, he waited to cross that invisible line before he and the others jumped out of the train into safe territory.

My mother had stayed behind. Someone had to pack the boxes. Besides, she wasn't in hot water like my father was, an ill woman who hadn't peddled the capitalist mindset so dangerous to the Communists. My father could wait things out and prepare the way for her to come. Still, my mother needed to find ways to evade questions from the authorities about Dad's whereabouts. Feigning apathy, she would tell them, "You go find him for me. He just left me. He does this quite often." Ten days later, Mom joined my father in Berlin. Finally, Mom and Dad could come to see me freely. Those early days spent with my parents were such a joy. Dad got the OK to build a small home in Bonn-Duisdorf. Mom delighted in little Fritz, and I smiled with a grateful heart every minute I spent with them.

But, combined with the joy of seeing my family again, I felt a bittersweet stab in my gut when I saw the letter from the consulate just a few months later. I had received my passport and could book a berth on the Queen Elizabeth, but it also meant leaving behind all I had known.

My parents and I had been reunited only to say goodbye once again. The tearful goodbye was almost more than I could handle. There were still so many unknowns, so many new situations, and I would be facing them without many of my supporters.

Dad met me in Munich as Fritz Jr. and I boarded the train to Paris. Stoic and stalwart as ever, Dad let me know about the things to pay attention to. He locked me in a crushing embrace before leaving us on the train, continuing to stare at us as we were whisked away. Fear gripped my heart. I only knew Germany, Austria, and Poland; now, I would be crossing an ocean.

Instead of the darkness I would have normally let into my heart at such a goodbye, I turned my face to the west. The trials and tribulations that had taken us away from my homeland were tinged with a golden light. We had surely been led by a guardian angel. It was like a light that propelled us along our way, pushing me into a future I had never expected for myself, coming from a past I'd never be able to fully put behind me. The journey was scary. The country seemed so vast, and New York so big. Would we find each other?

The day we arrived at the New York Harbor, we saw the Statue of Liberty's arms outstretched to welcome strangers. The emotions, the pain that can hardly be described, were whisked away by the inviting nation that stood before us. On April 8, 1951, my son and I set foot on American soil. Awaiting us there, a smile plastered on his face, stood Fritz. Behind him was a 1936 Ford, a car he'd driven from Wisconsin to pick us up.

My life was here now. I had come home.

LEADING WITH PURPOSE

So many of us feel the sting that comes from a difficult transition. My transition was slow, fated. For me, the 2010s marked just the middle point of my employment at Target, but it was a time of reinvention. I had found the faults in my previous leadership, and I was determined to make a difference. I was doing things I had never done before. I was now baring my soul to the people around me. Yet the nervousness I felt had given way to the zeal of connection.

I started seeking out opportunities to take on more speaking engagements. I've always loved people, and the thought of opening myself up seemed exciting, exhilarating. I started with the inner circle of my work environment and gradually moved on from there. Soon, it became easy to find speaking engagements.

At the beginning of my career, I was relatively alone. Not many women work within the technology sphere, and it became increasingly lonely the higher up the corporate ladder I climbed. I was used to seeing mostly men in my field. When computer science had first taken off, women had jumped on board, but this had suffered a steep decline. By 2010, the percentage of women working in technology had dropped to around 18 percent. Fifteen years later in the US, women still represent only 27 percent of the roles in the computing field.[1]

I had frequently thought of myself as an outsider. Not only was I a woman in tech, but I was also a leader. Many people who think of traditional business boards miss one key feature in the image: women.

---

1 Janine Lee, "Breaking Down Barriers to Belonging for Women of Color in Tech," *Harvard Business Review*, August 9, 2024, https://hbr.org/2024/08/breaking-down-barriers-to-belonging-for-women-of-color-in-tech.

My determination to be dedicated not only to my career but also to my family set me apart. It's incredibly common for most people to prioritize one over the other, and I often found myself not relating to many who didn't share the same struggles to balance the two.

But this uniqueness was a rare advantage. Perhaps, if many women didn't stay within IT and computer science because of the difficulties of juggling life and work, I could be an anchor. If I could inspire one person, one woman, to follow her dreams while not sacrificing who she was and what she believed in, it would be worth it.

Some years ago, I got the opportunity. My former assistant was struggling to make a decision regarding her work and family situations. She had just started a family, and it was becoming increasingly hard for her to maintain her previous lifestyle. She wanted to move out of her executive assistant job and into something more aligned with her long-term career goals.

We sat down and talked about possible future directions. She was incredibly bright, and our successive conversations let her know just how much potential she had. Through my consistent support and our many discussions, she eventually got a job she had never thought possible. She went from thinking she couldn't balance being a mom and having a career to switching her career significantly and quite successfully.

We still have conversations to this day, and she reminds me of the advice I gave her all those years ago: "Burn your candles … Life is too short to save them. Reach for the stars. You can do whatever you put your mind to!"

Seeing individual success like that lit a fire in me. It was like a switch had flipped when I reached outside my inner circle. It was amazing how much enlightenment I was starting to feel in a position where I had once felt so isolated.

Before I knew it, I found myself before ten thousand audience members, delivering a highly technical keynote at an industry-leading tech conference. IT was the field I had built my career around, so I'd been invited to speak at this important event. The bright lights and echoing cacophony on a stage many times greater than any I'd previously occupied were challenging, but that stage would also prove to be the entry to my greater sense of purpose.

Though I'd spent years developing my expertise in IT, I was also deeply invested in the people around me. When I saw people's reactions that day, I recognized I had more to offer them. I became less focused on highly technical business or computing topics and more engaged in helping others grow. When I urged people to look within, the souls of those hiding their true selves seemed softer, more willing to bend. So, while as a technical leader in these meetings, I expressed the importance of building the right culture, I also wanted people to absorb the importance of building each other up.

Instead of being merely a talking head on a subject that had many speakers, I shifted toward greater authenticity. Since then, I frequently ask, "On a scale from one to ten, what's your overall job satisfaction? Is it trending up, trending down, or flat?" It doesn't truly matter what the number is. The point is to start thinking more intentionally.

I had already seen the mistakes in my own life and the damage that had come from my actions. It might have seemed uncomfortable to mention all my failures, but the act of helping people by sharing my personal mistakes and life lessons made me feel like I could, perhaps, help them. I started looking for opportunities to talk to people after speaking engagements. On many occasions, I would intentionally ensure I was the last to leave just so I knew I wouldn't miss the chance to talk to everyone. I craved connection. I wouldn't let any opportunity pass me by. The amount of time I had spent separated emotionally from my own team had given me the boost I needed to become more involved with others. I might have only seen some people once, but I loved their stories.

This change of mindset not only influenced the people who attended my talks but also actively changed me. As I spoke more about intentionality and personal progression, I started to see those aspects more in my own life. Instead of rushing home to complete chores, I became more present in conversations. Instead of just going through the motions of making it in time to pick up my kids from school, I found opportunities to support them in sports. I was more present, seeing more than ever before.

Over time, I realized a universal truth: We are the guardians of our own progressions. In the grand scheme of things, we all exist on a giant chessboard. We often think that we're designed to go one way or another, do things the way that has been ingrained in our minds. But what if breaking out of that mindset was as simple as intentionally understanding your place on that board? Your mind and your thoughts are your own. Don't become the chess piece that somebody else moves across the chessboard.

EMPOWERING EVOLUTION

It's easy to feel small, even insignificant, in everyday life. Those feelings of inadequacy often come from a weary soul. You might be searching for a way to contribute to your job, make yourself more heard at home, push yourself harder than you've ever gone to improve your community. The erosion of our resilience over time can put us on autopilot.

But those experiences can be the anchor for someone else. The people I meet on my travels aren't aware of the impact they have on other people. Do you see your actions as inconsequential, almost robotic? When our actions become more intentional, they suddenly have consequences—you start to move mountains. That is the power of a PMA.

I've found that building cohesive teams is one of the most worthwhile accomplishments you can achieve. And it's incredibly easy to do. The more you start taking control of your own life, the more opportunities begin to appear.

Personal fulfillment comes from learning to live outside of yourself.

The needs of others start to become vitally important, and naturally, you grow as well. Life becomes drastically more satisfying when you're keeping others in mind.

So much of life is about beating you down. The feelings of loss, both personal and professional, the sting of failure—the fear of an uncertain future may make us feel like we are standing at the bottom of a staircase with steps too high to reach. In a world completely isolated from others, that height may be too great.

But look around you. No one is ever truly alone.

That first step might require a boost from a spouse, parent, even a coworker. Sometimes, that leg up is all you need to propel yourself to success you've never seen before.

That first step to empowering the people in your team when they're lacking direction or feeling uninspired can be intimidating. But it's often the priorities of their leader that make them so. You need to ask yourself, *Are people or deadlines more of a priority?* No matter where you are, no matter how far you climb, people should always come first. Big companies, small companies, and everything in between all revolve around others.

When I tell the people on my team that I want them to work me out of a job, I mean that if I have done my job well, I have empowered them, and I have created an avenue for them to develop and take on more. When I am not needed, that means they are performing at the top of their game. I want everyone else to do the same.

Everyone on your team has unique tools to aid them in creating a cohesive success. Your job is to help them develop new intellectual tools to help them succeed outside the workplace and within it. Empowerment is the greatest tool of all.

A HOME BASE RENEWAL

My newfound empowerment to help other people came at a cost. I was feeling freer than I ever had been, yes, but I found myself becoming busier than ever. I started to travel internationally for my job while speaking, which also required more local or domestic travel. It became difficult to fit everything in. Balancing my responsibilities meant more time chairing community organizations, spending more time with my family, pushing myself at work, and maintaining my personal health. My frequent travels meant that I couldn't put in as much effort to maintain my home.

Organization is vastly important in my life. Having things ordered in my home in just the right place clears my mind. Knowing I can easily find anything that needs to be within my reach keeps me grounded, leaving my mind free to think of other things. As with most other highly organized people, my system depended on my frequent attention to it. And I suppose—I suspect I followed the stereotype that is true for many women who run their households—I believed that the best way to do something quickly and to do it right was to do it myself.

As a matter of habit, I found myself paying the household bills, preparing our taxes, taking my boys to school and daycare, doing the laundry, and making sure everything was in order. When I felt myself falling behind, I simply told myself in that same robotic language I had come to know and love, *Get your to-do list done, Kim.*

But over time, I found myself slipping from maintaining everything I wanted.

Was I losing a part of myself? Was I giving too much and perhaps putting too much on my plate? This wasn't outside the realm of reason. I frequently put too much on myself. But was that really anything new? I had already been through so much that I told myself I could do it. And no one was telling me to stop.

In the back of my mind, I found myself becoming somewhat resentful. I had grown up with a certain ideal for myself. I knew I could get anything I wanted as long as I worked hard. Nothing is free. You have to work for things, and you need that mindset. But it wasn't as though my husband was incapable of helping. Was I truly making the right decisions?

It came as a revelation when I brought this up in a private conversation between my husband and me. It was the first time we really discussed what our roles were at home. Surprisingly, he didn't expect me to be a superwoman. I simply saw things that needed to get done and took the initiative, but he was more than happy to lend a hand. And he did.

Perhaps I wasn't subconsciously aware of how much guilt I would feel by letting part of my workload transfer to someone else. I had secretly wanted help for so long, but it had been my job to take care of people. When you take a bit of the burden off yourself, most people don't tell you that it takes some mental gymnastics to accept that help.

I'm sure so many other people feel the ache of letting go. Most of the time, that sense of letting go has nothing to do with the death of a loved one or the loss of a career. Sometimes, it's necessary to grieve over the things most people would consider small. Letting go of a part of yourself, even one you didn't realize you were holding so tightly, takes a period of adjustment.

But that period of personal loss opened me up to something quite extraordinary. I began to take closer notice of myself. I developed certain external strengths and intrinsic behavioral characteristics through my years that were entirely unique. When a small burden was taken off me, I climbed mountains elsewhere.

I expressed my creativity in a variety of new ways. I learned to share the general management of our household with my husband. I outsourced our tax preparation. This allowed me to become the general contractor for the home we built when my two older boys were very young. I even returned to baseball as a coach, coaching for my sons. I'd let go of something that I felt was an intrinsic part of me, but maybe that control had been holding me back. And though it hurt, I found a lot of joy in letting go of things that didn't work in favor of things that did.

LEARNING TO GROW

I frequently wonder to myself why people stop growing. Many people, as soon as they end their formal education, take pride in feeling as though they've learned enough. What a strange brag. Life is a continual learning experience, whether that comes formally or not. For my part, I frequently like to challenge the typical, and just last year, I graduated with a degree in executive coaching. Instead of a burden, education has become a way for me to tackle the "why not?"

At the same time, many of us feel lost in our own personal education. We were told for so long how to study, what to study, and which direction we should go. So many of us reach a point where we are simply satisfied with what we have learned and are fine with the prospect of strictly learning by coincidence. But that kind of thinking stunts our curiosity.

Perhaps that is why there's a stigma surrounding learning to learn. For many of us, it seems like we should have gained that skill already. We went to school, put our heads down, and read out of the same textbooks. Reteaching ourselves to learn for our own self-growth is difficult, but it can be one of the most rewarding experiences we'll ever have.

Mental Expansion

There's nothing quite like the desire to learn more.

Often, that desire starts with a shifting mindset. We face challenges, not problems. That particularly nasty quandary you're facing has a unique solution that is, perhaps, designed to test you. Instead of thinking about it with a defeatist attitude, slow down and be creative. How can you think about this from another angle? How can you move that chess piece to another position? If you constantly feel stressed, try breaking down the root of your stress and filling it with something constructive, such as reading a book. If you have difficulty maintaining a budget, come up with unique and creative rewards for when you meet your goals. If you're creatively blocked, try going for a walk.

I find myself diving into frequent fancies of strategic thinking. It's a great way to creatively express myself. In fact, the artistic expression of strategic thinking is what makes each of us unique. So, instead of reaching for your phone when you can't find the answer to the problem, consider finding your own solution. You can accomplish nearly anything with an "I can figure it out" attitude.

When just starting out, get a leg up. There are so many ways to try new things. Often, the strategic tools we find most helpful are found in the experiences of someone else. Henry David Thoreau found solace in simple living, spending two years on the banks of Walden Pond. Sometimes, that mental relaxation is exactly what I need as well. It's amazing the inspiration you find within the pages of a book.

Strategic Learning

Have you ever found yourself jealously looking at someone else's life? Perhaps they had the opportunity to go to the university they wanted to attend the most. Maybe they happened upon a business strategy that launched them into exponential success. Often, this doesn't occur by happenstance. The people most blessed with abundant opportunities actively sought them out.

We live in a remarkable time. There was a point in history when it was nearly impossible for someone with limited finances to rise above their station. Living as the poor son or daughter of a blue-collar worker may have limited their options. But today, there are so many opportunities to learn. A simple Google or AI search can provide thousands of cheap or free ways to learn. After the pandemic, online courses became more popular than ever. Today, you can learn without ever leaving the couch.

Sometimes, it's just as simple as using different tools. Bit by bit, piece by piece, the telescope was created. The basic design magnified distant objects weakly. Galileo refined the telescope by using a series of lenses and mirrors to focus bending light. Most of the time, our own problems are also solvable with the addition of new insights, new tools.

When I was first diagnosed with MS, I lost much of the use of my right arm. I found myself using my left arm much more often to compensate. My nondominant arm, the left, became much stronger and more useful. Now that I've regained the use of my right arm, I see the value in exercising the muscles you don't frequently use. It has now become my goal to write legibly with my left hand.

Strategic learning is about improving bit by bit. You'll find yourself becoming more self-sufficient all the time.

Collaboration

Imagine the first few lines of a brilliant tapestry. If you're looking at it up close, you might see a combination of vibrant colors woven into a faint pattern. But, when you zoom out further, you start to see the story unfolding. The unique colors blend to form a broad picture. When weaving your personal tapestry, you're merely reproducing the vibrancy of people's collective life experiences. As beautifully as you could weave your own tapestry, you could never synthesize the same stories, share the same brilliant colors, of unique lives.

Our personal growth serves as a valuable tool for the advancement of our community. The opportunities we pursue to grow are only made possible through the support and presence of those around us.

I'm frequently approached by people who ask me how I got where I am and how I manage to juggle it all. It's a broad question, and one I can't answer without mentioning all the people who helped get me there. The purpose of growing ourselves is to lift others. I don't care one whit about titles. What we should truly focus on is how we can better understand the people around us.

It saddens me to see how fearful some are to reach outside themselves. They have so much to offer, so much to share with others. When we share our unique skills with others who have complementary attributes, it can create magic. The tools we learn, the strategies we develop over time, should help us create a culture of empowerment. The patterns of our lives aren't complete without the vivid array of the stories and experiences of others.

EDUCATIONAL TRANSFORMATION

Some years ago, I got the itch to try something new again. During my career, connections from all over the world relied on my guidance. It only made sense to start thinking about other ways to acquire skills. I didn't have the time to get another degree then, but universities frequently have seminars and short educational programs. My company had recommended a continuing education certification course from Harvard, and I simply couldn't pass that up.

The course focused on unconscious bias, taking a deeper dive into self-reflection and how to lead successfully in a global world. I wanted to see the full economic picture. There are so many angles to what's happening around the world. My goal was to come out of that training knowing a little bit more than I did before about how to inspire people across the globe. All the while, I would be staying in dorms again with fascinating people.

Getting a certification from Harvard was a tremendous opportunity. I had not gone to Harvard when getting a degree, so the certification program gave me an excuse to live on campus and learn something new from a variety of new people. More than anything else, it humbled me significantly.

Ultimately, though, the experience was much more about the connections I made than anything else.

In my travels around the world, I noticed that there's always a place tourists usually just pass by. The people living in those places are incredibly vibrant. Because my classmates came from all over the world to join me in that Harvard certification, I got to learn from them directly. Those cultures that differed from mine provided a new perspective on leadership, but they also connected me with people halfway across the world in ways I'd never expected. Those very real people explained their struggles, successes, and everything in between.

A noteworthy man coming from the Middle East particularly caught my attention. His country had been embroiled in conflict for decades. It wouldn't have been unexpected to think that he would be saddened, even angered, by what he had experienced. After my time at Harvard, he reached out to everyone again. He was exceptionally positive despite it all. He had so much on his plate, living in a place with so much unrest, yet he met us with a smile on his face.

I'm very blessed to live where I do in the world. I'm also incredibly lucky that I come from brave people who were willing to escape oppression and start a new life. They granted me these opportunities. It's not uncommon to think of people around the world one-dimensionally. Without experiencing people's cultures and personalities as a whole, we often lose perspective. We discuss other countries' peoples as though they are merely statistics far removed from ourselves. It's hard to connect with cultures so far away.

But the beauty of educating ourselves about other people is that it doesn't rely on the size of our pocketbooks. Gaining an appreciation for the people who have come before and even the current population can come from vibrant stories woven into books. On occasion, we may discover that someone from a distant corner of the world has settled right in our own neighborhood. The journey of another's story could only be a few steps away.

I still have a picture of the people I spent time with while getting that certification. I still speak with them. Though some of us live thousands of miles apart, we're connected on a much deeper level. And none of that would have happened without a deep desire to learn.

5

Streamlining a Brighter Future

INGE IBS

America seemed so vast. But, with Fritz here, sitting across from me in the diner, it was a little less overwhelming.

I brought the menu up to my eyes and scanned the long list of things to choose from. It was almost like a storybook! So many options I hadn't seen for years. Fritz must have seen my confusion, so he ordered us eggs, coffee, toast, and juice with a slight smile on his face. We ate, feeling a sort of relief to finally be with each other again.

Full but satisfied, we stood up to leave, but as I leaned against the table, my fingers came away sticky. Fritz explained to me that it was chewing gum someone had left behind. I contorted my face in disgust. Something like this wouldn't have happened in Germany, leaving bacteria behind for other people to touch. But perhaps chewing gum was a rite of passage, a sign of the times that I was becoming truly American.

The scenery whizzed by as little Fritz and I were whisked away by my dear husband to our new home. We traveled through New York and Pennsylvania, leaving the concrete and the smell of automobile exhaust in the dust and passing through fertile farmland. We passed through Ohio, traveling the freeways in the direction of Green Bay, Wisconsin. I found myself transfixed by the splendor of it all. In the back seat, little Fritz stood up and stared out with me. Back in those days, we didn't have booster seats. Luckily, little Fritz only went flying a couple of times when we slammed on the brakes or drove too fast across a particularly bad railroad crossing.

Finally, after nearly three days, we arrived. Brigitte, my friend from what seemed like a lifetime ago, had found us a place to live in, upstairs in the home of her parents-in-law—Clarence and Martha. With all the driving, little Fritz had temporarily lost the ability to walk. I had worked so hard to have him potty-trained while we were on the Queen Elizabeth, but it was like he had forgotten it all. As frustrated as I was, Clarence was greatly amused.

During those early days, I was cautious. In Germany, we had to be careful about foreigners. But the warmth of my new house reminded me of back home. Here, my family and our hosts would reminisce about the old days while speaking hopefully of the future.

Clarence and Martha had their own experiences with loss. They'd lost a son in Holland, shot down by the Germans. I felt a knot in my throat. "I'm sorry" was all I could say, my eyes welling up with tears. But Clarence and Martha replied with a sad smile, "You lost two brothers in the same war. That's why we have extra love for each other." It was a startling reminder of all that we had lost. We had all suffered in different ways, but we shared a commonality in our hearts. Perhaps it was this same experience of grieving that had given us greater compassion for all kinds of people.

Some months later, I received a letter from my father, begging me to come home. My mother was in the hospital with hepatitis, and Dad was devastated. The little money we had scraped together hardly seemed enough to transport both me and little Fritz back to Germany, but God was good to us. It took seven days for us to make the trip, and we were back at my parents' side.

Things remained grim in East Germany. Dad had taken several jobs, running different offices, just to apply for better quarters for them to live in. Money was tight. So, leaving little Fritz at home with my mother, I took a job as a clerk and appointment setter at a newspaper. It was a blessing to help them again after so much time had passed, but Fritz was always at the back of my mind.

After some time, we scraped together enough money for our return home. I yearned for Wisconsin, but Fritz had found a job in Minneapolis, Minnesota.

Just like my parents, we found ourselves moving frequently. Minneapolis had many opportunities, which was perfect for little Fritz, but we shifted seemingly endlessly. It was a few more years until we would settle down in a house, something we could call our own, just days before I gave birth to my second son. Though small, Fritz had the wherewithal to turn that home into something grand. He expanded the kitchen and made room for visitors over time. Mom and Dad visited us, and even Fritz's parents came to see us and the children.

I hadn't expected the greeting we would get when we moved to the United States. Our cultures were so different, and part of me wondered if those differences would make an impact. But God was good. Everywhere we turned, people were good to us. We shared stories of war-torn lives, and my friendships with exceptional people proved the catalyst for my parents' frequent visits. When my youngest son was baptized, we even found a service performed in German, thousands of miles away from my home.

As the years progressed, we crafted a life for ourselves. Fritz began to read about farming. I quit my job as a factory assembly worker to go to beauty school. Finally, in 1962, we found the perfect farm.

The old house needed refurnishing, updating. But with a good few days of scrubbing, we made it comfortable.

Those summer days lazed by beautifully, taken in from the huge screened-in porch. The first winter, we prepared by stacking hay bales around the house to keep in the warmth. The boys played in the snow, coming back reporting on pheasants inhabiting the cornfields. In those early days, we waited by our new phone to hear about the snowplows. Life wasn't easy, but it came with a kind of satisfaction I can't relate to anything else. We had built something for ourselves. We had seen everything taken away from us: our world, our livelihoods, even our families. But watching my sons playing in the beautiful countryside of Minnesota, I felt a happiness like no other.

I never stopped feeling homesick for happy days gone by. My children brought me untold joy, but it saddened me to know they would never know their uncles. Each of my children—little Fritz and Tom—carries one of their uncles' names, a testament to the mark they left on my heart. When I saw them playing outside, enjoying the freedoms of America, I couldn't help but reminisce, thanking God for the beauty of overcoming.

OF COBWEBS AND CONVERSATIONS

Sometimes, that simple life my grandmother had seemed the most beautiful in all the world. My own sense of peace came, paradoxically, from the damaging effects of inner turmoil.

I'll never regret the first years I spent in my career building my skills and growing as both an employee and a mother. I've often felt it's my duty to make sure that everyone is happy. I will trade the loss of sleep for an organized house. And, back in those days, I did what I had to do to keep everything running, to keep everyone satisfied.

For a time, I worked on call as a computer engineer. I'd really gotten the hang of it, and I found myself becoming increasingly valuable to my company. During emergencies, it was my responsibility to find a solution, even if the problem occurred in the middle of the night. But I continued pushing forward. It was just what you did. I come from a hardy German background, which means that you do the hard work, no matter how much of a toll it takes on you.

Problems needed solutions, and there was no reason why something as inconsequential as a lack of sleep should get in your way.

Despite it all, I was determined to maintain my relationship with my family. My grandmother was one of the most important people in my life, and we shared weekly letters paired with Wednesday calls. I needed the support from her. She had been through so much herself, and her constant words of encouragement sometimes seemed like the only things that could get me through the week. She was always extremely positive, and I figured, with a life like hers, if she could do it, I could too.

I felt it the hardest those first few years of advancing my career. I was flattered at the chance to take a somewhat demanding role. As a woman, I frequently found myself in the minority, even alone.

On the home front, I continued to toil away. I had grown accustomed to having things done in a certain order. I needed a strict regimen and serious organizational skills to maintain a life that seemed like it was moving far too quickly. Being a mother and a full-time employee has its downsides. Though I hadn't recognized it at the time, my mental health was slipping again. Once again, I was pushing myself too far.

Unsurprisingly, some things fell by the wayside.

I had known my grandmother's birthday was coming up for some time. Going to a party for her was important, especially since I didn't know how many she might have left. But life got in the way. So, on the week of her birthday, I sent her a letter expressing my regret for my upcoming absence. Unfortunately, the little things had piled up, and laundry and yard work needed to be done.

I looked forward to her reply, still regretful about the opportunity I would miss. When the letter finally arrived, I turned it over in my hands with a quick, bracing breath.

As the remarkable woman that she was, she gracefully understood. But her beautifully skilled handwriting gently chided me:

"Don't worry about the cobwebs in the corner. You're going to miss the conversation at your kitchen table."

I am so remarkably like her. She, too, sought an organized and clean life. She fought hard for what she wanted, always doing something, always caring for someone. Perhaps, in that moment, she recognized a part of herself in me that needed taming. And she was right. I was much too focused on work and being busy. I had forgotten to be present.

That letter, all these years later, still sits in my home office, a constant reminder to remain grounded and appreciate the present moment.

TAKING THE BACK SEAT

When we're young, life seems to go by so slowly. For many of us, we can't wait to grow up. But, when we finally do, time goes by so fast. The day starts; then suddenly, it's over. Years go by in a flash. We think we have time to do whatever we want to do, putting things off until the last minute or simply telling ourselves, *I'll get to it when I can* or *Someday, I'll have enough resources to do the things I want to do.* But then, those scattered dreams fall by the wayside.

Crushed dreams and ambitions are the result of dreaming of "someday." We often get caught up in things that seem so important in the moment but are so trivial looking back. That desperate attempt to keep the house clean and manage busy children distracts us from those truly unforgettable moments. Those days we spend, head in our hands, poring over the assignments given at work, constantly fearing that we'll never measure up, prevent us from looking at those moments spent with good friends at work. Hurriedly pushing your dog away because he or she was a distraction resulted in missing the moments you could have spent enjoying their company.

We might frequently tell ourselves we'll get to it eventually, but those times pass quickly. In the end, you might have a reputation for hard work, discipline, or any number of other admirable qualities, but did you miss what was truly important? The truth is, there are far too many things to do in life and not enough time to do them. The moment we start to push away the important things is the moment we start missing out on our own lives.

I often think of the simple phrase, "Saying yes to something means saying no to everything else." So, each time we practice saying yes, are we doing so with intention? Every time we say yes—whether to a meeting, a project, or even a casual commitment—we allocate that time, energy, and focus away from other opportunities. We could be saying no to rest, personal growth, or even the chance to prioritize something more meaningful.

So, what are we truly saying no to?

At the end of the day, there are mundane tasks that will always need to be done. If we fritter away our time focusing on those instead of what's really important, we'll lose our lives, becoming a tool for someone else's free time. Maybe it's time we put down the duster and the vacuum in favor of simply sitting out on the porch.

Of course, the moments you really need to take a step back are rarely clear. At too many points in my life, I found myself too burned out, too tired. I had put so much time and effort into things I saw as important, and I neglected myself. After a while, my diminished mental state and corresponding physical condition forced me to take a step back.

The letter I received from my grandmother—a memento of her love that I consider one of my most valuable possessions—was the sign I needed to prevent myself from going down a dark path. In the end, if you don't find the time to give yourself rest, your body will force you to do it. That gentle reminder for me to take a step back was exactly what I needed to keep me from doing more self-inflicted harm.

It's taking me time and patience to develop a system of fine-tuning my instincts. There have been more than a few times I've simply pushed aside my feelings of burnout in favor of simply pushing forward. I don't like to take breaks. I don't want anyone else to pick up the slack I leave behind. My version of a balanced life was making sure I could fit everything I needed to do in a single day.

But then, my mind would return to my grandmother's story. For as long as I can remember, she was always doing something. Yet she still found herself staring out the screen door, having a beautifully lazy Minnesota day, gratefully smiling at her grandchildren. A peaceful life comes from taking in those moments.

The transformation we go through may not seem dramatic. Sometimes, it's the simple gesture of letting go that really matters. We're becoming someone different every day by choosing to live life more intentionally.

I know that more than a few people feel the same way I do, filled with an innate desire to accomplish more. Yet I wonder if, perhaps, the endless pursuit of that worthy goal prevents us from living a life of true meaning with the people we love.

We may evolve into something we never expected. We become part of a story we hadn't planned when we were children. That transition is often small, guided by the power of a single decision. Yet it can happen at any time.

And perhaps it's a beautiful thing to simply sit out on the porch on a lovely summer day, breathe in a big breath of fresh air, and smile at the flowers you hadn't noticed before.

A CAREER SWITCH FOR PERSONAL GROWTH

Toward the end of my tenure at my first job, I sat down with my husband to have a serious discussion about our future. Over the few years preceding my resignation, I had climbed the corporate ladder, had two of my sons, and had moved across various disciplines within IT. My life had already radically changed, and some part of me knew I couldn't stay.

I have always striven to grow at every point in my life; call it an internal obligation to myself. As much as I wanted to believe that I could stay in the same position forever, it soon became clear—with the significant mergers and acquisitions—that my husband and I needed to diversify and expand our industry knowledge.

Our conversation came with mutual consent. Both of us had felt like we needed to have the conversation. We both agreed that we had outgrown our current positions and needed to find something new. Since we had started at the same company, it only made sense to spread out, to try to diversify our employment in case of mergers or acquisitions.

My husband was exploring new opportunities, and though I wasn't actively looking, I was recruited by Target. They were looking for someone who had a background in IT, and my experience with leadership in my roles made me a unique candidate. It was an opportunity too good to pass up.

As destiny would have it, my husband had already applied to Target. He, too, was a valuable asset, and they were eager to have him join the team. Unexpectedly, we ended up in the same position we had been in before: working at the same company and, ironically, starting at the same time. But it was a gut call—and the right one: The positions at Target were in the best interest of our independent careers.

Target allowed me to stretch my managerial muscles. Though I had experience from my previous job, Target was new and diversified. I would be leading a larger team with a focus on operations. It was the first time I found myself shoulder to shoulder with senior leadership in retail, an entirely new industry for me, where the pace of technological innovation was fast.

But, just as it had happened many times before, I found myself losing sleep. I was just as busy as I had always been. To me, that was the mark of a hard worker. Not to mention, the people in this company had a significant reputation to uphold. Target is one of the biggest retail corporations in the United States and has a significant reputation for delivering a strong customer experience, and everyone there knows it. My position was a coveted one, as were the positions of my colleagues in senior leadership. Many of them not only felt the urge to succeed but also gained a significant rush from achievement. Just like I had been when I first entered Augustana University, I found myself on the same level of achievement as others. I wasn't unique in my staunch desire to produce as much as I could. Many of us had sleepless nights. It was just another part of the job.

Up until then, I had found myself relatively alone in that endeavor. Many who reach a high executive level naturally work longer hours.

To some at the highest levels, a machinelike attitude toward completing tasks is the only way to rise to the top.

But the results were eating me alive. I wanted to do more, but I was always sucked into the same monotonous work structure. Many people at high corporate levels don't have kids without significant help at home in a dual-career family because they simply don't have the time. I hadn't opened up to many of them. The only glimpses of their lives I saw were at mahogany desks. I felt myself becoming increasingly alone all the time. Yet my grandmother's letter retained a profound influence on the continuation of that lifestyle. I started thinking that perhaps I was putting in too much work. I wanted to keep up with everyone else around me, but just how realistic was that?

What most people won't tell you is that the most valuable asset you have is time. When you reach those high corporate levels, it becomes increasingly difficult to tear yourself away from work. You start to miss those moments. For many of us, we get stuck in the same loop of producing, producing, producing. When we get home, we follow that same template. The leaders in the industry, the people I look up to most, achieve more while having more time to do other things.

Remarkably, there was something I could do. To cope with my responsibilities, I developed a system for success. I kept myself focused on important tasks while delegating the things that didn't need to keep me occupied. As it happened, it was possible to have a life outside of work.

A VIEW FROM ABOVE

So many of us get sucked into that same vicious cycle. We work until we're burned out, give ourselves enough time to take only a quick breath, and then we're back at it. We stay up too late because we "have the time to get a little more done." We stay at the office long past the time anyone else is there because, "If I don't meet my deadlines, something really bad could happen." We scarf down food in the kitchen while our family eats at the dining room table because, "It's my job to keep everything clean and orderly for my family." The endless droning of time, pushed by the drum of a monotonous heartbeat, forces us to live in that same robotic style just to stay afloat.

But that pattern is contrary to true development. We leave a small part of ourselves behind every time our inertia of productivity keeps us chained to our desks. The minute we start seeing ourselves as merely the bearers of a burden or simply duty-bound to fulfill someone else's dreams is the moment we need to step back and take a look at ourselves.

Luckily, many of us have instances in our lives when we can streamline processes. Instead of relying on last-minute notifications, we can set up calendar events to stay in a routine. We can declutter offices, leverage automation to make it easier to find information, saving us from wasted time searching. Even something as simple as getting our groceries delivered instead of going to the store can save us a lot of time. We're not merely forced to stay in a terrible situation in the hope that it will eventually play itself out. But it takes time and true reflection to reach that point.

Identifying Your Focus

Let's, for a moment, take ourselves away from the present. Imagine yourself on a mountaintop, staring down at your life. You may see, at various points in the road, true moments of happiness and other moments of pain. At first glance, it may seem as though your life has followed a meandering course. Maybe it feels as though you don't know where your priorities lie.

But if you take a step back and really analyze what lies before you, you'll start to see patterns. Those moments when you were truly happy followed certain activities. Maybe you see yourself smiling the most when you were around family. Maybe you were traveling to unique locations and meeting different people. Maybe you found the greatest joy in pursuing a passion you once believed would be your purpose in life. Whatever the case, everyone has something that makes them truly happy.

Oftentimes, we get caught up in doing the small things and forget about who we truly are. Those moments of happiness, those times when you felt yourself grow the most, lead you back to who you are. But we can get lost in following the wrong paths or pursuing things we only thought we wanted.

I found myself losing who I was when I focused too much on my ultimate goal. I got lost in the details. I lost sight of what truly made me happy and my purpose in life because I wanted to achieve a goal I told myself I needed to accomplish. All along, what I wanted most was to work with people. It took me several course corrections and the comments of some of the most important people in my life before I made that ultimate shift. It came down to intentionality. I was responsible for my own unhappiness, which meant I had a way to fix it. I just focused on the wrong things.

So, instead of jumping from point to point, take a view from above. And don't forget to take a snapshot so you won't forget.

The Gelling Process

There were many points in my life when I felt a sense of urgency to change things. Sometimes, I like to attribute that to my intentionality, but other times, it's just a gut feeling. When I left my first job, I knew I wasn't pursuing the direction I needed to. When my life was out of balance, requiring the help of my grandmother, somewhere in my gut, I knew she was right. The direction I was going in simply didn't fit who I was.

It's all too common for people to question if something is right yet push forward anyway. The expectations of family members, coworkers, or even yourself can make you feel so at odds with yourself that you start to question your true purpose. In those moments, so many of us want to give up. That should be the sign that our processes simply aren't gelling with who we are.

Of the many people I talk to, a lot of them have similar problems. They have become so focused on their goal, so determined to reach their destination, that they've lost part of themselves. When was the last time you showed your personality while working? If your answer to that question is "Never" or even "What personality?" it might be time for an about-face.

Most people stop progressing because they have chosen processes that don't allow them to exercise unique solutions. So, instead of fighting who you truly are, embrace it. That snappy, feisty person inside you prevents wasted time. That low-key, laid-back person you told yourself to ignore may have more connections than anyone else around you. That eternally optimistic PMA of yours may just be the catalyst for inspiring thousands. Who you are deep down isn't a liability; it's your greatest asset.

Making Time

I find myself relating closely to people who feel driven to achieve, committed to setting and surpassing goals. Many who, on the outside, seem as though they are controlling often only exhibit those traits because they don't want their responsibilities to slip. They feel so duty-bound to protect others that they prevent themselves from letting go. It's taken me many years and hard lessons to feel otherwise.

For many people, but especially for women, we feel it's our duty to take care of everyone else. We see people around us, who seem to have it all made, juggling family and other responsibilities with a smile on their faces. But behind many of those smiles are fears of disappointing others.

I offer a solution that may seem counterintuitive: Put yourself first. This seemingly selfish approach is anything but. If we put ourselves first, we ensure mental stability and happiness, which allows us to be the best mom, coworker, leader, and friend to others that we can be. A project that takes twenty hours instead of the projected two may be a symptom of a larger problem. Often, time management is difficult because we're so burned out that it's taking us ten times as long as we originally thought. Instead of pushing forward, we should be taking a step back. There will always be times of stress. There will always be more to do. But if you find yourself saying, "I simply don't have the time," make the time. Being kind to yourself is often the one task we leave undone.

AN INTERNAL TRANSFORMATION

Balance has been the most difficult thing to achieve, yet the most important thing I've tried to accomplish in life. Perhaps that's why I talk about it the most when I mentor others.

Trying to be perfect is an endless pursuit that will ultimately take you down. I'm such a people pleaser, just like my grandmother. When I look back at the stories she told, I wonder if she ever learned to let go. I don't know if she ever put herself first. What I do know is that she imparted to me a simple phrase I constantly carry around with me: Don't sweat the small stuff.

When creating your own future, when going through experiences that are difficult and push you, it's hard not to get derailed over the small things. A bitter look from a coworker, a subconscious slight by a family member, or a door slammed in your face is only a single moment. In the grand scheme of things, not everything works out.

But if I were to leave a legacy today, there are moments in my life I'd want the next person to know. Some things were very difficult. Some things taught me, rather painfully, that I'm not invincible. But I gained a confidence I never would have had if I hadn't reached outside myself. If I hadn't let go of some of those more useless tasks, if I hadn't focused on the future I envisioned for myself, I might not be the person I am today.

Each of us has those moments of self-reflection. Sometimes, they come in the form of devastating losses, and sometimes, you're lucky enough to have someone tell you directly. Those uncomfortable reminders from some of the most important people in my life have now become my most treasured moments. Though difficult for me to hear, my grandmother's gentle reminder that I had lost my most pressing purpose in my family was just the ticket I needed to help reorient myself. These reminders told me to take a step back and realize what's really important. They've helped define who I am. Without them, I might have been lost forever, pursuing things that just don't matter to me.

For anyone looking to find their purpose, to strengthen their resolve by streamlining their life, I have a simple suggestion: *Sit in silence.* Perhaps your true purpose is hiding under the noise of a busy lifestyle. You might find that, if you cut through that noise, there's a part of yourself just waiting to be happy if you stop for a moment and listen.

6

Radiating Individuality

INGE IBS

We continued to host Mom and Dad when they came to visit from Germany, which was steadily becoming more frequent. I had built a life in Minnesota, but family seemed endlessly far away. Every time we parted, it became a little more difficult.

In 1965, I received a letter. My parents felt like coming again. To them, Minnesota, though far away, may have seemed like their home back in Germany. Before the war, of course. When I checked their tickets to see how long they would stay this time, I found a pleasant surprise. Mom hadn't bought return tickets; they would be staying with us from now on! But when they arrived, it was bittersweet. Mom and Dad had to leave Germany because of the Warsaw Uprising.. That beautiful House of the Sun, the house I had always thought of as the most beautiful in all the world, seemed lost to us forever.

The growing number of people in our house sent us a clear sign: We needed to upgrade. It was hard to bear those wintry seasons. The draftiness of our old house, even somewhat slowed by the modifications we had made, let the chill in. We had always dreamed of building a farm, cultivating our own crops, and caring for our own animals. Perhaps now was the time. We didn't have a lot of money, only what Fritz could scrape together from Honeywell and what I had made from the beauty parlor, but it was enough for God to grant us a loan.

What had once seemed to vanish from memory was now returning in the form of Fritz's house plan. I could hardly believe my eyes when I saw luxuries, such as big windows, appearing on the blueprints. We did much of it ourselves but hired a few builders to make the work go faster. After less than a year, we finally had heat, electricity, water, and bathrooms. We moved in that January. As a test, Mom turned on the faucet to be greeted by warm water. She cried out in excitement. Warm water out of the faucet after years of shivering under blankets to remain heated? It seemed like a miracle. That night, we could barely sleep. Despite the snow carpeting the ground outside, the warmth of the house kept us cozy.

We entered a new season of routine. Fritz continued to work at Honeywell while I set up a small salon in the basement of our new home. Between the cattle escaping and the constant stream of people that entered our home, I found myself always up and moving, washing, and cooking for six people.

I had found another family outside of the one inside my own walls. Building my church community became vastly important. It was from our pastor, Kurt Gust, that we learned more about the Warsaw Uprising. He had also come from that area. In a strange way, it was almost like that news was a blessing. Mom and Dad knew no English, so our German community, found in the rural countryside of Minnesota, was almost a miracle. We became close through our stories. The lives gained and lost, the fears of the future now completely changed, cemented a feeling of camaraderie I'm unsure we could have obtained without our shared German roots. Though I didn't realize it at the time, I had developed a talent for bringing people together.

I suppose there was a part of me that always knew it was my destiny to take care of people. I was always in a position to take care of people. Though we never had much, we always had something to give. I formed a Bible study group every Tuesday and invited fellow parishioners over to visit throughout the day. As luck would have it, we were able to afford a small pool. We kept it open for anyone in the parish who needed it. My sons grew up knowing a family greater than the one they'd been born into.

I could barely believe my luck when, in April of 1970, my family grew further. My little Fritz, the one who had come from Germany with us, the first to experience the upheaval and subsequent beautiful building of our lives together, had found the love of his life, Pamela, and I gained a daughter. Pam was so clever, and it only made sense to invite them to stay with us when we found out she was pregnant.

When their little daughter was born, it was like a breath of new life into our home. Soon, Kimberly followed. It was like I was reentering a dream. My mother, always more blissful in the presence of children, cared for them with me, always glad for their presence, especially in the last few years of her life. She lived another eight years with us all. Those last few years of her life, those filled with smiles and giggles, will always be a blessing to me. They're a sign of God's goodness, even in the hard times.

It felt like a dream to introduce that new generation to something that meant so much to me. I still cooked those same German recipes. My little grandchildren got endless pleasure from watching me in the kitchen. Being able to make a dish from practically anything is truly a gift that is born out of wartime. It's a skill I didn't want my grandchildren to miss out on. So, though there were moments my heart ached when teaching those young girls how to cook, it's something I would never take back.

It was during those years that I started to realize something about myself I hadn't previously considered. I had seen so many people come and go, frightened of the lives that lay before them. To me, though those fears will never completely go away, I've always had the gift of knowing that things would work out. Throughout it all, strong beliefs and positive attitudes are contagious. I've seen lives changed for the better by acknowledging a higher power is at work in each of our lives.

After everything I'd seen, why wouldn't I keep a smile on my face?

A GAME OF UNDERESTIMATION

I'm often compared to my grandmother. Maybe it's because we had that same sense of positivity about us. The more I work with people, the more I realize how much of a gift that truly is. Like her, it's given me the perseverance I never would have otherwise had.

After having three boys, I realized I probably wasn't going to be able to return to softball in the same way. I had coached a little bit of high school softball, and I had started coaching T-ball as a volunteer, but I wouldn't be returning to my roots in the same way. But through my sons' interest in sports, I got to relive my glory days a bit. At the age of nine, my oldest son became interested in baseball. I don't know if it was because I rubbed off on him or if something about the game drew everybody in, but I was ecstatic. My interest in baseball coincided with my recent desire to get into giving back to the community. It also gave me a great excuse to spend more time with my sons, one of the balls I had been trying to balance for quite some time.

As my two older boys grew, they became less infatuated with the idea of baseball. They shifted to lacrosse, a sport I knew little about. Still, I did my best to support them in their new endeavors. I found myself cheering for them from the sidelines.

But my youngest son found joy in the same things I had. Baseball became something we shared, and I could be more involved than I was in lacrosse. Because I knew my way around softball and baseball, I quickly became a parent head coach for youth programs and eventually high school boys. After so long away from the sport that had started it all, I was back to coaching full-time in the summer.

As luck would have it, the American Legion Baseball team needed a coach for last year, and I was asked to take on the role. The players on my team would be competing against boys their age who specialized in baseball. They would have the chance to compete with people all across Minnesota. As a former college softball player, I felt a unique drive to profoundly inspire the next generation. There's something about a team sport that brings out the sportsmanship in everyone, and I couldn't wait for another opportunity to give that to a new generation.

The first days on the field were much like any other. I had been coaching for twelve years, so I knew the ins and outs of competition. I guess I shouldn't have been surprised when I didn't see any other women out on the baseball field. I was coaching a competitive league for boys aged fifteen to sixteen. Most of the boys were bigger than I was.

At one of our first tournaments, we got skeptical stares. Just before the game, I was approached by the umpire and asked where the head coach was. I cleared my throat, looked him square in the eye, and said, "That would be me."

I looked over at the other head coach, who had raised his eyebrows. Under his breath, he whispered, "I've never seen a woman head coach before." Then, turning back to his players, he signaled for them to start their warm-ups. They entered the field, and the coach hit a few ground balls. It's the standard way to warm up: They were going through the motions, the mechanics, of the game.

I'd heard a little bit about this team before we made it on the field. This team was one of the best in the state. The majority of the boys on the team only played baseball, and they played it year-round. On the flip side, most of the boys on my team played baseball as their second or third sport, and only in the summer months.

On paper, we were at a disadvantage.

But, shrugging off the look the coach had given me just as I had done so many times before, I returned to my players to start their warm-ups. Our warm-ups were somewhat unconventional. The most important aspects of my team involved putting in the mental work. I work with people around the globe, and I've maintained the habit of building strong teams and a culture where we can give each other feedback and talk about things we need to work on. I wanted the boys to work as a team. One of the greatest approaches we had was to sit on the bench and talk first: What's our approach to this game? Are we dialed in? Where are our heads? What strategy can we use in this game?

When my players headed out on the field, they were more than ready.

I watched with pride as my team beat the other team. We, all of us, had been the underdogs. But, in the end, that hadn't mattered. My team had worked together, capitalizing on those long weekends and the short amount of time we'd had to build our team. I could see the other team's fans looking at us in disbelief. While there's something inherently satisfying in that, it paled in comparison to the joy I felt when I welcomed those boys back to the dugout.

All in all, we won the tournament. Our city had been in that tournament for thirty-six years, and they had only won it four times. It was a big success for all of us.

But when I look back at those days, the win wasn't the most important part to me. One team member approached me during the season and told me how much he respected me. A mother contacted me and told me how grateful she was that her son had grown while I coached him. Those smiles and mindset shifts meant the world to me.

I've always tried to instill a PMA in everyone who works with me. I like to think it's a contagious quality anyone can inherit. But leaving those breadcrumbs behind means I often don't see how other people change in the long run. My methods were anything but traditional, but I saw a change in those boys I'll truly never forget.

THE STRENGTH WITHIN

Those points in time that create your strength are often hidden in the moment. At times, you may be begging life to simply give you a break, not realizing those are the exact moments you needed to become the person you are.

Looking back, in the moments I was coaching those boys, I certainly hadn't thought I was the most influential person on that team. Far from it. In most cases, I feel like I'm simply an observer witnessing someone else's strengths. But that ability to step back and support others, build faith, and encourage people to find the best in themselves is perhaps my most cherished strength. It's a strength I inherited from my grandmother, and one I don't know if she recognized her whole life. But to me, that strength meant more than anything.

I frequently come across people who believe that their unique personalities are a hindrance to their progression. Some people feel that they're too talkative or not talkative enough, or they're too open with their feelings or too closed off. Some feel that they're too ambitious, while others only wait on the sidelines. "Who am I," you might say, "to perceive my personality as a strength?"

Doubting yourself is easy. It takes true courage to accept and project your traits for your own good. Soar with your unique strengths.

The parts of ourselves that we feel are the most troublesome often give us an advantage. I'd be lying if I said that the sideways glances and comments of incredulity I received on the baseball field weren't disappointing. But I've frequently been the underdog, and I've received harsher criticism than that. But in the moments after, the moments when my team members came up to me and thanked me for my contribution, I realized the importance of maintaining that strength.

But what are you doing to make that well run dry?

So many of us feel like we are stuck in an endless cycle of overwork. Sometimes, the days seem so long, and getting away to express yourself becomes a faint memory. That kind of burnout can make it seem like you're running on overdrive. It's a common phenomenon among people who are looking inward.

Perhaps surprisingly to many, I have found the best way to build strengths—or even just to recognize them—is to take the time to give yourself a selfish examination. We often confuse strength for weakness. In those moments when we feel that despair has taken hold of us, that we can't go on, that we must submit to surrender, those inner strengths are most prominent. The truth is, if we really step back and analyze who we are, we might start to realize the parts of ourselves that make us unique.

One of the hardest lessons many of us have to learn is that doing too much can hide our unique strengths. When I first started coaching last season, a recent shoulder injury meant I couldn't hit ground balls. So, to let myself heal, I could not physically participate with the boys as I typically would. But that setback led to an opportunity. It forced me to flex, to bend. It forced me to develop my unique style of coaching, which focused more on mental rather than physical preparation. I encouraged my players in ways other coaches didn't. I had to think of strategic ways to make the most out of an unfortunate situation. It's not something that many other coaches would consider a strength, but it became vitally important to our strategy.

Recognizing a lack of invincibility is sometimes the greatest gift we can give ourselves. No one is meant to go through life alone. We only rise through our connectivity with others and our ability to say no when we realize we can't do something.

That period of healing can take a long time.

If you have already gone so long working as hard as you can in a seemingly endless state of burnout, those dreams you had when you were younger can seem out of reach or downright unappealing. But when we give ourselves the time to heal, those parts of ourselves can come back.

Reaching that state of mental and physical clarity doesn't have to be fleeting. The biggest enemy of our souls is the suppression of who we are. If we start to embrace what makes us truly unique, it becomes much easier to maintain enthusiasm for life. Despite what the world throws at us, we can face any dilemma with a smile on our faces.

PROMOTING TRUE INDIVIDUALITY

It's easy for your personality and individuality to become lost in a corporate setting. Being part of an organization can sometimes make you feel like just another cog in the machine, where individuality is overshadowed by a uniform label.

On another occasion with thousands of participants, I discussed technical topics with a variety of people, a broadcast that reached multiple countries. I had reached a point in my career where I had become well known not only for my background in IT but also as a team builder and promoter.

When I exited the stage, I was greeted by a woman. The experience wasn't entirely out of the ordinary. I frequently met with people after I gave my speeches. But before I could go into my usual handshake and conversation, she quickly complimented my shoes.

The flattery took me aback. Most people I talked to weren't interested in that sort of thing. In fact, *I* usually wasn't interested in that sort of thing either. I smiled politely and thanked her for noticing.

"I'll bet working in Target marketing is fascinating. You've done an excellent job in their recent campaigns."

Part of me wanted to look back at the stage I had just come from. It seemed strange that she hadn't noticed I was the keynote speaker for an IT conference when I had just come off the stage. Not knowing what to say, I merely smiled and said, "Thanks." I knew that I didn't typically fit the bill for an IT professional, but this was becoming something of a trend.

A couple years earlier, I had gone to an invitation-only enterprise architecture conference in Palo Alto, California. I had wended my way through a crowd of people to sit at a table with fellow IT architecture leaders at prestigious organizations. Standing next to the table, I had greeted some of the legends who sat there. They'd all made a name for themselves and looked like the typical IT heads of department: white men. They had complimented me on the event, congratulating me on the skill it took to put such an impactful agenda together.

"Oh, I'm not the event coordinator," I had said, and then I'd sat down at the table.

They had shared a glance among themselves. It's true, I hadn't looked like the typical IT guru. They had expected someone who looked a little more like them to lead that very technical team.

Though I had experienced things like that in the past, I still hadn't been able to help noticing that those men hadn't thought I belonged there. They gave no active pushback, but I had still felt an unspoken pressure to stay silent. It became a real challenge to be an active participant. Someone who looked like the event coordinator had sat down at their table and had led their highly technical discussions. It was a problem I was highly aware of. In many cases, it might have been easier to simply sit back and listen to the conversation.

But where would that have led me?

The experience encouraged me to speak up more, to share my unique point of view and expertise. I knew that I belonged, so I raised my head a little higher. I wanted others to recognize me. Shining confidence is an invaluable asset.

Often, those moments of pushback gave me the greatest opportunities for growth. I had been underestimated, yes, but I had the advantage of coming in as an unknown, as someone who would challenge the norms and give people something to think about.

EMBRACING UNIQUENESS

There's something empowering about being true to yourself. It's telling yourself that, no matter what happens, you'll find a way to push through.

On many occasions, I've found that the way out of a particularly difficult situation comes down to acknowledging and playing off my unique characteristics. I've used innovation to find strategies for complex problems. I've remained adaptable and flexible to changing circumstances. But perhaps best of all, I've remained positive with a good sense of humor when things looked really bad. Being an underdog in those cases was an advantage. I could learn what worked for the people who typically fulfilled a role and what didn't. Then, I could incorporate my own style.

But it's hard to reach that step. Cutting through the noise created by others requires real skill. It comes down to truly believing in yourself and what you have to offer. The first step you take away from believing that you can't do something is the first step toward creating a truly authentic strategy.

The Positivity in Underestimation

Criticisms sting. They always do. But what if you could use them to your advantage?

I often think back to my grandmother and what she experienced through a very difficult life. How had she not given up when bullets had rained down on her while she cowered next to a train of mercy? How had she not said "No more" when she was close to starvation in East Germany? How had she not curled up in a ball of self-pity when one of her first houses in America had become so cold they had to stack bales of hay next to it to keep in the warmth? It all comes down to a shifted mindset.

My heart has never been as tough as my grandmother's. I look up to her more than nearly anyone, so when I fail, I have to ask myself, "She didn't give up, so why would I?" She gave me the unique opportunity to compare myself to a true legend. The expectations I set for myself are compared to someone who went through so much more than I ever will. Those expectations for myself have set my standard.

You'll never live up to the expectations someone else sets for you if you don't feel a certain connection to them.

I've found that the best way to push forward through the pain is to have expectations for yourself and never settle. In reality, you can do whatever you set your mind to. But it takes courage to prove that to yourself.

When a coworker or superior approaches you with heavy criticism, don't back down—use it as an opportunity to prove your resilience. If you're struggling with a difficult project, push forward with determination. And when you're facing a loved one who doesn't understand your position, hold onto your resolve. Show yourself that you can rise above the challenges and exceed every expectation. You decide to give up. You also decide to stand strong. So, pick strength every time.

Letting Go

It's OK to give up.

That phrase is nearly seen as taboo, but it could mean the difference between engaging in the things you need versus remaining in a slump created by your persistence. Not all personality traits are valued the same way by everyone. Sometimes, it's better to give up in favor of something that works better for you.

It's easy to resort to apathy. Time goes by quickly, and soon, you will realize that you've been going through life on autopilot. Most people go through something like this, some of whom never recover. It's a crisis of meaning, a crisis of purpose. Your mind is taking you far away from your current tasks as a way to escape. In short, your priorities aren't completely aligned.

Letting go of those tasks and priorities you used to bolster your purpose for so long can be gut-wrenching. Many times, those priorities and expectations come from someone. A mother who lives vicariously through you, a friend who wants to do something they never could, or a manager who wants something for you that doesn't resonate with you all provide external anchors that keep you in the position you don't want to be in. Fulfilling the expectations set by other people sometimes seems like you're giving up a little part of yourself.

In reality, you're sacrificing something you want to be in favor of something that you are when you give up on those passions that don't give you purpose. The step away from the things you thought you wanted or that others wanted for themselves is one of the hardest steps you'll take, but it will be worth it in the end.

Encouraging Uniqueness

So many people have stepped out on their own with a dream in their hearts to pursue their uniqueness, only to be shot down over time. Oftentimes, we are the ones sabotaging ourselves. Why is it easier to deny what we're good at than to embrace it?

Finding your inner strengths and living by your talents can feel boastful. Sometimes, our self-deprecating nature drives us to deny our unique strengths. We feel obligated to be humble. But that feigned humility is woefully misguided. It's not prideful to accept our values and use them as strengths. It's a conscious choice to be more confident in ourselves.

But life has a way of bringing out who you are. Time after time, you'll find yourself in situations that demand your unique characteristics and traits. For all the people who struggle to maintain the status quo, perhaps it's better that you simply let go. It could be that life is trying to teach you something. What better time to bring yourself to the challenge, the whole challenge?

THE STRENGTH THAT FINDS YOU

I have always felt a deep sense of responsibility to ensure that those around me feel safe, heard, and supported. Throughout my life and career, I have witnessed societal shifts in how we discuss integrity, justice, and advocacy—especially in moments that test our collective values.

In a world where stories spread at lightning speed, the challenge lies in distinguishing truth from assumption. We live in an era where headlines are often more compelling than facts, and narratives—true or not—can take on a life of their own. Tabloids and social media amplify this effect, sensationalizing difficult moments and, at times, distorting reality. But this pattern isn't limited to national news; it plays out in our workplaces, communities, and personal lives.

Gossip is one of the most destructive forces in human interaction. A rumor can spread like wildfire, and once it does, there is no undoing the damage. I have seen firsthand how words—unverified, exaggerated, or simply false—can ruin reputations, divide teams, and create lasting harm. Too often, people assume that if a story is being told, it must be true. But believing something just because it's repeated does not make it fact.

I have seen the lasting impact on individuals whose truths were dismissed for years, only to finally find their voices heard. I've also seen cases where accusations were made and later proven false—yet the damage was already done. In both instances, lives were irreversibly altered. These realities remind me that accountability must come with a commitment to fairness, careful consideration, and due diligence.

The difficulty lies in discerning fact from fabrication. We want to trust the narratives we hear, especially when they fit into the broader cultural conversations of our time. Yet, when people rush to judgment without evidence, they create collateral damage that cannot be undone. I have seen individuals ostracized because of whispered accusations. I have watched how reputations, built over decades, can be dismantled in days simply because a compelling story overshadowed careful scrutiny.

It is unsettling how quickly people align themselves with the loudest voices, assuming that consensus equates to truth. But I have learned that true wisdom comes from pausing, from questioning, from reserving judgment until all perspectives have been heard. The strength to resist the pull of the crowd is not easy to cultivate, but it is one of the most important skills a leader—or any individual—can develop.

There is a quiet strength that comes from standing apart from the tide of public opinion, especially when that tide is fueled by gossip rather than evidence. It takes resilience to navigate these complexities with both conviction and compassion—to assert individuality while extending grace. It takes courage to stand by those in need, even when it comes at a personal cost. It takes clarity to seek facts, even when emotions run high.

The pressure to conform is immense. It is far easier to go along with the prevailing narrative than to challenge it. But easy does not always mean right. I have had moments in my career when standing for what I knew to be true meant standing alone. I have faced criticism, skepticism, and even anger for questioning assumptions. But every time I have chosen to pause, to listen, and to demand fairness, I have known I was acting in alignment with my values.

Leadership, at its core, is about integrity. It is about making difficult decisions, about advocating for what is right even when it is unpopular. It is about ensuring that we do not allow fear, bias, or convenience to dictate our actions. True leadership is not found in those who simply follow the crowd; it is found in those who have the courage to stand when standing is extremely hard.

This is not to say that accountability is unimportant. Quite the opposite—accountability is essential for justice, for progress, for trust. But accountability without fairness is simply another form of injustice. If we are to build organizations, communities, and societies rooted in true integrity, we must commit ourselves to a higher standard of judgment. We must teach ourselves and others to pause before believing, to seek evidence before condemning, to remember that every story has multiple sides.

Words carry weight, and how we use them matters. Whether we choose to spread truth or speculation defines not only the impact we have on others but also the integrity we carry within ourselves. There is great power in being the person who chooses thoughtfulness over rashness, fairness over bias, and truth over assumption.

It only takes one person to stand up against the tide of misinformation. It only takes one person to advocate for nuance, for fairness, for patience. It only takes one person to make a difference. And that person can be you.

The ability to think critically, to step back and assess a situation with a clear mind, is one of the most valuable skills we can develop. It allows us to lead not from emotion alone but from wisdom and perspective. If we allow ourselves to be swayed by every wave of public opinion, we risk losing the ability to discern real truth from constructed narratives.

Standing up for truth and justice does not mean ignoring wrongdoing—it means addressing it with a level head and a commitment to justice rather than knee-jerk reactions. It means allowing space for context, for investigation, and for understanding. It means holding ourselves to a higher standard of thoughtfulness and refusing to let gossip and half-truths dictate our beliefs and actions.

This responsibility is not just for leaders or decision-makers. It belongs to all of us. Every conversation we engage in, every assumption we make, and every conclusion we jump to contribute to the culture we create. If we want to live in a world where integrity and truth prevail, we must each be willing to pause before we judge, to listen before we assume, and to stand firm in our commitment to integrity.

7

The Power of Progress

INGE IBS

On Valentine's Day in 1976, my youngest son, Thomas, and his new wife tied the knot. Soon, they had children of their own, a wonderfully fast-growing family. I had started with two sons, but, before I knew it, I had two daughters as well. Everyone in the family blessed me with beautiful grandchildren. It was a period of peace, one of tranquility I hadn't often experienced while young.

But while my family was growing at an exponential rate, I soon found them slowly leaving my presence. First, my parents passed away, then my son and his new wife moved away with the two daughters they had brought with them, and then my final son also moved away. It was still vastly important to me to maintain a strong connection with them, to constantly keep in touch, but I felt myself missing them more than I could bear.

My beloved Fritz stayed closer to home after the children left. Instead of traveling miles to go to work, he found jobs around Maple Lake. He farmed. In general, he kept himself busy. It was a chance for us to spend more time together now that the children had left home. With so many people gone, it was a blessing for anyone to come see us. Fritz's mother, Oma Ibs, came to stay with us shortly after my mother passed. She was a welcome addition who helped to pick up the pieces of a broken heart.

At first, life seemed to pass like a trickle, then a stream, then a flood. Before I knew it, Fritz and I had been married for thirty years. At that point, we started to feel ourselves slow down. I still remember the look on Fritz's face when he sold off his cows one by one. He had named them all, and it was heart-wrenching to see them disappear. But it was clear: We needed something, someone, to bless.

We decided to join the Annandale Evangelical Free Church in the latter half of the 1980s. We spread the word of the gospel and soon opened our home to Bible studies. We prayed together to bless the mission of building a new church. Our beautiful home, built by my beloved Fritz, became the center for more church activities. We had space to accommodate people who needed a place to stay, so our home became something of an open house. Missionary speakers came. Interim pastors stayed with us. At times, we even opened our house to beautiful spectacles made by those in our church group that involved painting sceneries, sewing costumes, hammering, and practicing.

I was constantly surprised at how easy it was to get involved in helping others. The poor were always in need of food and love, and we constantly spent time with others, teaching songs and the gospel. But the cause was much bigger than what was in our small hometown. It seemed so much more important to reach out to people and provide aid, much like the aid I had received all those years ago. Then, before we knew it, we left the United States.

Fritz was ever a companion to me as we made our way to Haiti in 1986, 1987, and then in 1988. We found so many across the poverty-stricken country who were looking for help and support. Several members of our parish offered humanitarian aid, which we delivered.

On occasion, we brought some of the Haitian people in need back with us, giving them an idea of what the United States was like. Hosting was a blessing we could provide to some. It was the start of our never-ending devotion to helping others, and I felt a particular love for the Haitian people.

Just before our fortieth anniversary, Fritz and I heard news from Europe: The Soviet Union, after splintering for so many years, was finally coming to an end.

The possibility of the unification of East and West Germany seemed so surreal. The people in East Germany had suffered so much under the oppression of Communism. The horrifying rule that resulted in death, fear, starvation, and more had been a reality for so many. It felt like the veil had finally lifted from a time of oppression. Nearly a century of riotous command had yielded a country so broken that many of the people still felt the shame of calling themselves German. But this was a step in the right direction. For the first time in a long time, it seemed as though we were moving closer to peace, farther away from the history that had so wrecked much of Europe.

The wall went down in Berlin on November 9, 1989. It was like two halves of one heart had come together again. Families that had been separated by a tyrannical reign and the oppressive nature of a large cement wall could finally hug each other again. Friendships that had been destroyed over forty-five years of separation could once again flourish.

But it meant something even more special to me. Perhaps, for the first time in nearly forty years, I could return to my hometown of Dresden.

Fritz and I headed over to Dresden shortly after the fall of the Soviet Union's regime. After the fall of the Soviet Union, my parents' old house had reverted to our name. I was the last surviving member of our original family, so it fell to me to do something about it. There was a part of me that felt nervous, traumatized. It had been my home, the location of so many happy years, yet my beautiful city had been bombed so terribly that much of what remained from my youth was still rubble. The process of rebuilding and restoration after German reunification was a vision that had only just begun. Though there was hope in the eyes of the people who still lived there, it was clear the past half century had been miserable.

I quickly dragged Fritz through my once-beautiful city toward the hill where my house stood.

Miraculously, it was still intact. Because it was set apart from the rest of the city, it hadn't endured the same terrors. But the House of the Sun had lost its splendor. It hurt my heart to see the beautiful home now dilapidated. Still, it was the nicest home there.

The question remained: What to do with it? Though the land was important to me, I had no need for it. I had created a life in Minnesota, and all the family I had left were there.

As I admired the beauty of the old house and contemplated the sadness that had driven me away, I happened upon some of the people from the old days, family I hadn't seen in years, still living in Dresden. They had long loved the House of the Sun. The house had been empty for quite some time, and it was condemned. It needed a lot of work. But it seemed only right to sell it to them.

Smiling, I filled out the paperwork to transfer ownership. I sold the house to them for a fraction of what it was likely worth. It didn't matter to me anyway. We didn't really need the money.

I still remember the look in their eyes as they gladly accepted. After all the hardship, they had plans for rebuilding. It was an unusually large house, which meant it could easily be split into a fourplex, which was what they intended to do with it. It was beautiful seeing their bright faces as they took ownership of that once-beautiful house. It was almost a mercy, after all that had happened there, to see it turned into something truly beautiful. One by one, the connections I had to Germany were slipping away. They became mere memories, which is as it should be.

When Fritz and I returned to the United States, we had a little more money in our pockets. But it didn't feel right. We had been lucky. We had built a life away from the war, a life that was beautifully preserved in the legacy handed down by our family. So, looking at each other for a moment, we both nodded. We were in agreement.

It wasn't much money, but it was enough to build an orphanage in Haiti. It didn't take much soul-searching to do it either. The people there needed help much more than we needed money. And I would receive those precious pictures, worth so much more than mere dollars and cents.

THE PAIN OF PROGRESSION

In the mid-2010s, I felt the need to move on from Target. I'd been there a long time, and I had learned so much. I had spent a whopping decade of my life there. I owed a lot of my growth to Darren Matthews and a conversation he likely doesn't remember but that still holds a place in my heart. My work at Target wasn't challenging me like it once had. I knew in my gut I had to move on.

Building relationships had become central to my personal brand. The relationships I had built at Target will, I hope, last a lifetime. But the majority of the personal connections I had made at Target didn't translate to culturally diverse teams. Target was one of the biggest retailers in the United States, and I had dipped my toe in the water briefly by expanding to Canada and leading teams in India, but it wasn't the same as working at a global company.

Something about incorporating other cultures was exciting to me. I still hold my early experiences visiting India as some of the most profound I've ever had, and I could only imagine how much greater my experience would be after seeing more of the world. Maybe that's what made me look outside of my Target bubble.

I had recently been approached by a larger organization, one with a global influence. But I had some reservations about my move to Cargill. There was a certain fear of letting go of a job that had given me so much, but maybe that was mostly because of the fear of the unknown when moving to a larger corporation. It would give me the step up I needed, but it wouldn't be easy.

The transition to new work wasn't difficult. Like many times before, I continued to work in IT. One of the biggest differences was that Cargill had a more diverse portfolio with broad global outreach. I was the head of IT operations, and I would work with teams from all over the world.

As luck would have it, Cargill's headquarters wasn't far from my home. The company was founded in the latter half of the 1800s, shortly after the American Civil War, and it had grown to become one of the largest privately held companies in the world. Cargill spanned many different industries, and the complexity of the business intrigued me.

I'd been in plenty of corporations that had wide-reaching influence, but there was something different about this one. It was exciting, new. And it could greatly expand my experience.

But I had worked at Target for ten years, and it had given me so much experience and many friendships.

Over the years, I've come to find that difficult changes are the ones that help you grow the most.

I had found that the ever-shifting landscape of Target had become something like muscle memory. The experiences I had there were easy to navigate. This change was daunting, yes. But if I were to stay in my shell, constantly encountering the same challenges, what sort of legacy would I leave?

It was time to stop sweating the small stuff. It was time to move on. I needed a new experience, and my new journey was just getting started.

THE SMALL STUFF

I'm occasionally approached by people who ask me how to keep growing. They want to know how I got to be where I am today and if there's any advice I could give them for their own journeys. I always answer the same way: What are you afraid of?

So many of us make it a habit to become overwhelmed by the little things. That job interview that didn't go how you wanted it to, that relationship that ended when you thought it would last forever, and that midterm exam that you failed all seem like the end of the world at the time. But perhaps those things weren't meant for us after all. They're merely devices to test whether we will continue to push when things get rough.

Too often, we box ourselves into circumstances that keep us trapped in a type of stasis. Becoming successful is difficult. It requires the drive to expand our horizons and look for stretch opportunities. Oftentimes, that stretch comes with a little discomfort.

Think about it this way: Imagine the constant stress your body is under to grow when you're little. When you're born, you're only a handful of pounds and a few ounces. Over the next eighteen years, your skin is forced to stretch to accommodate growing bones and muscles. At times, it's painful. In the end, you might be left with stretch marks, scars, or sagging skin—signs of positive growth.

So, what would you do if you could simply stop that growing process?

One could argue that avoiding growth might translate to more ease, less pain. The mental and physical scars you'd accumulated during your intense season of growth would perhaps cease to exist. But would that stasis be worth it?

It's that positive development that keeps us going. One of the greatest lessons I ever learned from my grandmother was the ability to keep a smile on my face, even when it's difficult. Her struggles were so much more difficult than mine. The losses she felt were excruciating in comparison with the small number of losses I have dealt with. If she could handle all that, why can't I persevere?

Keeping a PMA is a surprisingly difficult lesson to learn. I've needed a PMA to become much more aware of myself and what I can handle. At times, I've looked back and chided myself for my closed-mindedness. But that, too, is just another step on the road.

When I look back at my life at the end of my days, I want to see a life of running. I want to see myself running toward the things that seem scary. I want to see myself running toward those misty bridges where I'm not sure where my next step will land. I want to see myself running toward problems that seem too big to solve. Whatever happens in the future, I'm sure I won't see myself backing away from anything. The growing pains are never too hard to overcome. The opportunities are never too big to push me away. Whatever happens, I want to know I gave my all.

A GLOBAL TRANSFORMATION

The road to the next chapter of my life was exhilarating. As I transformed myself, I was also leading transformation on a global scale.

At Target, I managed complex teams, but at Cargill, the challenge expanded exponentially. My first major leadership role was optimizing IT infrastructure operations. A few years later, I was entrusted with building a new shared services operating model from the ground up. The scope was massive, with countless stakeholders, diverse teams, and high stakes.

My colleagues spanned continents and cultures, operating in different time zones and speaking multiple languages. Some felt like next-door neighbors, while others were literally half a world away. My job was to unite them, streamline operations, and drive large-scale transformation.

But cracks quickly emerged.

The complexity was unlike anything I had faced before. A model that looked flawless on paper buckled under the weight of global diversity, cultural nuances, and deeply ingrained ways of working.

People felt disconnected. The strategy, though designed for efficiency, wasn't resonating with those who had to live it every day.

I realized I had to evolve the strategy—probably more than once. I needed a new playbook, one that balanced structure with flexibility, global vision with local adaptability, and efficiency with human connection.

So, I got to work—not just transforming the model but transforming the way I led.

I'd learned from years of working at Target in large groups that the feedback of my employees was among the most important conversations I could have. I also knew how important it was not to let only my way of thinking take charge. The employees were looking for something out of their company, and I wanted to provide it, even if that meant restructuring the model two or three times over.

It took some time before we settled on a final plan that satisfied most people. The new solution would require buy-in at every level. Luckily, that meant I could reach out to teams worldwide and hear their feedback. I quickly became close with as many team members as possible to ensure they felt heard and to see that their suggestions were implemented.

When the war in Ukraine broke out, I felt a sudden pang of fear in my gut. One of the leaders with whom I had worked closely lived near the front lines in Russia. It was my job to make sure everything ran smoothly, which included the well-being of my employees, but there was much more to it than that. This woman had become my friend, and as the descendant of a war victim myself, I couldn't help but feel the worry with her.

She soon confided in me that her sons had been called to war. It seemed like something out of a nightmare. The war had broken out over a cause she had no control over.

It was not in my job description to reach out directly regarding her family. Maybe that was why she gave me a stiff, "It's fine," whenever I asked about her family. If she said anything else, political forces might have intervened. She would smile back at me and then tell me that everyone in her team was performing well, and so were her sons, so there was nothing to worry about.

Though I oversaw so many people, there was a part of me connected to each one of them. The changes we implemented on a business level were essential, and adjusting expectations and responsibilities became simply another aspect of our roles. But seeing the world through their eyes was an experience I'll never forget.

There's power and purpose, and working with people, guiding them through the good and the bad, is hardly easy. I grew, not from the expansion of my personal duties but through my connections with the incredible people who touched my heart worldwide.

THE POWER OF OVERCOMING

So, how do you grow through those hard times?

An element of my German culture meant I was raised to push through the hard times. From a young age, I felt it was my duty to put in extra effort to make sure that everything worked out. I worked odd jobs to make extra money. I was strong for family members when we were going through tough personal experiences. I stuck by the people who meant the most to me because it was in my blood to do so. If you'd asked me how I pushed myself to grow, I would say I did so naturally.

Some of the hardest times in our lives mean the most for our personal growth. The times when we were too timid to raise our hands and present a solution to a problem, the times we found ourselves sobbing on the bathroom floor because we felt alone, and the times we felt so burned out we couldn't possibly carry on provide the decisive moments that help define who we are.

But, contrary to common belief, those learning experiences make up a small part of true growth. It's also about the intentionality we put behind our actions following those growth experiences. If we never look back and recognize the lessons we learned, we'd be forced to learn those lessons all over again. That self-reflection, the most uncomfortable part of the journey to relive, is the most important part of overcoming, learning, and growing.

Magic in Intentionality

At some point, most of us have experienced burnout or the overwhelming desire to give up. Sometimes, it comes when you've worked eighty-hour weeks for too long; sometimes, there are too many losses in your life to bear; and sometimes, the burdens of life just seem too heavy and hard to overcome. Progression seems like a foreign word, even abrasive.

The key to healing comes through intentionally incorporating a PMA.

It's also the key to growing and moving on. If you're too busy focusing on your success, you don't have time to worry about the small things.

In times of extreme stress, I find myself lingering in conversations at the kitchen table. My friends and family have a beautiful talent for erasing a lot of my worries. And in the times I don't have them near me, I carry a notebook in which I can express my thoughts and feelings without stepping away from what I'm doing. I can put a pin in my emotions for a short time while actively acknowledging that they exist. And when I want to totally unwind, one of the simplest ways to do so is to just leave my phone at the door.

Too many of us are afraid to live life. As I see the years progressing, I see so many people trying to flee from reality. Reality seems so much harsher than the imaginary worlds that most people can enter by simply turning to their phones. But perhaps that is because many of us aren't shaping our realities to fit our needs.

It's quite amazing, really, when we start dreaming of a reality we can achieve. The losses seem to sting less, and the successes seem more prominent. All of this comes down to an intentional life. The progression we make is in our hands and always has been.

A Mind Unafraid

At times, people look at the confidence of others and only wish that they, too, could one day have that same level of confidence. I'm frequently approached by people who are looking for the same thing. With so many people separated so far apart and with fewer interactions than ever before, confidence is becoming a rarer and rarer skill.

But confidence is a waiting game.

Think back to a time when you really struggled with something. It could be a difficult skill you had to acquire or a traumatic experience you had to get through. Though it seemed hard at the time, you always got through it. It became a skill you could add to your arsenal, even if you felt the repercussions would stay with you forever. Confidence is a lot like that. You develop something over time that helps you survive in similar or even more difficult situations.

The hardest part is growing an independent confidence.

When I started my job at Cargill, I had a great team, but much of what I had to do required standing alone. This responsibility was one of the hardest tests of my confidence, but it was also the greatest builder. During the most difficult months, I learned to be vocal. Instead of letting others talk over me, I held my own and believed in my own strengths.

It's tough to be vocal. It's tough to stand up for yourself. But the moment you start feeling like you can let things brush past you without letting them affect you, you've hit a confidence marker. You've grown exponentially, and there's no stopping you from growing your confidence even further.

Embracing Loneliness

Many people who are looking to progress significantly aren't aware of how lonely it is. There's a reason there are only a few massively successful people. Quitting is infinitely easier than holding on. That loneliness can get to you over time if you let it.

But the myth of loneliness is that it requires a rock-solid foundation. Many of us feel like we need to have endured a certain number of hardships to hold out in the long run. But the truth is, we all have to start somewhere.

The fear of loneliness can keep us from starting our own initiatives, mostly because many of us are afraid of our own company. We don't want to confront the difficult thoughts we have about ourselves, and we'd like to be distracted from such trials. But those moments of silence are essential to helping you understand who you are and how you can overcome obstacles. It takes a great deal of courage not to feel sorry for yourself when something doesn't go your way. The first time that happens, it's painful. But you can't let those moments get to you. You have too much to offer.

Being lonely at the top is like standing at the top of the peak of a very tall mountain. When the wind blows, sometimes it's hard to stand your ground. But somebody needed to make that climb first so that they could pull someone else up. I'm grateful for the opportunities I've had to take on new and pioneering roles throughout my career, helping to create pathways for others along the way.

After a while, where once there was loneliness, there's suddenly an army of us standing at the top of that mountain. We've made it so much farther than we ever could just because someone was willing to be lonely.

CREATING A GROWING LIFE

I certainly didn't consider myself to be one of just a few when I started my first job. In fact, I had no intention of being lonely. But, in my senior year of college, I received a few job offers, one of which was in IT. I didn't think much of how it might shape my future at the time. The IT field had still been new back then, and I saw its potential. I looked into the job because it provided training that could give me valuable skills for the future.

What was then called St. Paul Companies, Inc. was the oldest company in Minnesota at the time. It focused on commercial property liability insurance and asset management services, fields that aligned with my business degree. Plus, it had a robust technology training crash course, which meant I could go into the company without a degree in IT. When I was selected as one of the potential candidates for the position, I was thrilled. It seemed like the perfect way to get started in my career.

I quickly learned, however, just how competitive this position was. I took a long aptitude test, where the primary goal was to find potential leadership skills. The company excelled at creating management. We went through a series of recruitment processes that were designed to weed out those who couldn't adapt as quickly.

It is safe to say that, at the time, I was far from the most qualified there. Some people had gone into IT in college and were far more prepared than I was. I was frequently astounded by my esteemed twenty-four peers with whom I started my training program, but I didn't let fear stop me from trying to learn with them and from them. Eventually, my hard work paid off. I started to get the hang of the basics of computer engineering.

But sooner than I would have liked to admit, I found myself at the bottom.

It wasn't entirely a surprise. I had business experience, yes, but this position was more demanding than that. I had made it farther than so many other people who had applied for the position, but it still didn't seem like enough. As my first shot at a "real job," it seemed as though it wouldn't work. But the company found that I had other skills that might be useful and was willing to train me to get me up to speed.

I often think back to that time and wonder what might have happened if I hadn't gotten that job. From that single decision to work in IT, my entire life changed.

So many jobs since have seemed like blessings. I've done so much, seen so much. When I speak to others who want certain jobs to grow and develop, I'm often surprised by how many people don't go for it. That daunting list on a job description seems to hold many back. But who knows? I always tell people to avoid looking at the description if it makes them feel like they can't do it. Most of us simply need the will to push forward. Who knows where I'll be in ten years? But I'm so excited to find out.

8

The Rewards of Risk

INGE IBS

Life moves along too quickly. In the blink of an eye, I find myself becoming increasingly alone. I'm more grateful than I have ever been before, knowing that my life has been in the service of others and that I've made a difference in my family's lives.

But where does the time go?

Instead of being a primary caregiver, like I was for so many years, I saw a significant change in my life. I was in more of a supporting role. I guess a tumultuous childhood never allowed me to believe that I would make it as far as I have. It's a mercy, a blessing.

Many of my grandchildren have grown up and have started lives of their own. In fact, I was delighted to hear when Kim said she had found somebody for herself. I was excited to see another generation coming soon. It was as though there was a part of Fritz and I being passed on, learning our stories, sharing our disappointments, rejoicing in our triumphs.

With Kim starting her journey, I found her coming to me to talk about it. It was such a significant change in her life, and what an honor it was to provide my own input. I looked back on the days I started my life with Fritz. Every time those conversations came up, I couldn't help but smile. "Just let him be right sometimes," I said as I gave her a warm hug. "It's never easy to include everything someone else is into who you are, so it's incredibly important to keep the peace. In the end, conflict isn't worth the energy. The little things don't matter. I didn't need to be right in everything, and you'll find a lot more happiness in realizing you don't need to be right in everything either."

After our conversation, I looked down at the ring on my finger, the one Fritz had given me all those years ago. I gently slipped it off my finger. It seemed only right that she should have it. After all, the joy it gave me to see the smile on her face was one of the best gifts I could ever receive.

With the prospect of my grandchildren having children of their own, I started to wonder how much time I had left. I started to think about my life, one so much longer than the lives of some of the loved ones I'd left behind. I like to think that a lot of what I have gone through already has made some impact on the people in my family. A tumultuous life is difficult to live, but it can be helpful for family members to see a bit of themselves in the past. I have always thought of the wonderful power I held, knowing where I came from. I had such strong roots, such a strong family, and they propelled me to experience a life blessed by a God who always looked out for me and to have a smile that never seemed to leave my face. It was the first time in a long time that I really started to think about writing down what I've done. I've always fancied myself a bit of a writer, so perhaps this was the perfect point to start.

As my immediate family continued to spread out, I felt comfort in participating in more church activities. My own guiding light in life didn't have to stop at an orphanage. Maybe I could start influencing people from around the world.

I attended a few Stonecroft conferences, several of which took place in Canada. The women in my church took me to several in the hope of strengthening our testimonies and participating in the mentorship of women around the world. I became increasingly surprised at how little I knew.

But, as always seems to happen, as my knowledge grew, the world seemed to get a little smaller. And the more people I met from around the world, the more I started to see the faces of loved family members everywhere. The life I lived wasn't unique. The war-torn families of ages past existed everywhere. I found myself unique in my happily ever after. Though life hadn't been easy, it had been filled with love. I had gotten to live a dream I never thought I could. All those days, long ago, that filled me with such fear were gone. All around me were the faces of the people I had come to love and the family I had helped to raise.

Fifty years on from marrying the love of my life, I was still in love with the people we had become.

OPENING GLOBAL DOORS

I sometimes wonder about the risks we take, not if they're worth it, but if we're too afraid to take them. Do the risks become smaller over time? Do we become less likely to achieve what we dreamed of years ago? Some of us have found a home in one position or another and feel it's our duty to stay there until we die. The longer we stay in any position, the harder it is to move on. Perhaps that's one of the reasons I chose to shift in my career.

My move to Cargill had many more opportunities for change than a simple update in employment. My time at Target earned me a reputation for departmental transformation, and it was one of the major reasons why Cargill wanted to employ me.

Working in IT has given me an avenue for exploring different business operations. I have helped companies with the planning, building, and implementation of IT processes. I made it a point to understand every aspect of IT. The extra years of work it took to study every phase paid off.

When I first started in my position at Cargill, I was met with a lot of praise. People had wanted a new, fresh look at typical IT processes. For a global corporation, one of the most difficult parts of integrating a global team is maximizing efficiency while organizing thousands of people. If you've had previous business experience and more than a few years of IT leadership, it's something of a dream role. The aim was to centralize IT resources, infrastructure, and services across multiple departments. This is a great way to reduce costs and ensure more consistent service delivery. If I was lucky, the processes I put in place would last for many years to come.

My first day on the job was by no means easy, but it was extremely exciting. When I got home, I sat at the kitchen table and pulled out a map of the world just to see how much of it I would get to see. Occasionally, I would run my finger over the different countries and think about the people I would work with thousands of miles away. There was a possibility I could interact with people who shared my roots. But, even more enticing, I could learn from people across the globe.

Yet, there was a part of me that started to feel a real fear about the decision. By then, I had developed a method for changing my perspective on fear: It was far more a tool to push me in the directions I needed to go than it was a deterrent from the possibilities. So, to overcome some of those insecurities I felt, I returned to what I knew best.

My first instinct was to implement the systems I had already used in years gone by. They were effective and efficient.

Unfortunately, I quickly realized just how complex the moving pieces in an international team really were. Target was largely a domestic operation. Most of the people had similar goals, similar aims. Many of us, if not all of us, had grown up in the United States, which meant we had the same work ethic and expectations for output. But an international team was different. I started to see roadblocks I hadn't seen before.

There was a part of me that wondered if I'd made the right choice. This was an exceptional risk. I was doing something I had never done before in a company that was largely foreign to me.

At some point early on, I found myself thinking back to my grandmother. In the years since she'd passed, she always seemed to be on my mind. My frequent visits with her had brought a sense of stability to my life. Now that she was gone, a part of me left with her.

But my grandmother had left a legacy I could only hope to live up to. She had been there through the good and the bad. She had fought hard for what she wanted. There was strength even in a simple memory.

Ultimately, it came down to doing what I do best: forming relationships. The technical part of me had wanted to take over and simply deliver, but the people person in me knew there was much more to it. I wouldn't let a risky proposition hold me back from such a staggeringly incredible opportunity.

POSITIVE RISK

So often in life, we're pushed in directions we never knew were available to us. It's almost like there are invisible winds that push us in the direction we're supposed to go. The new trajectories we have for life are exciting, riveting. They open doors to directions we're supposed to go in, as if everything that happens in life happens for a reason.

At many times in my career, the direction in which fate pushed me seemed difficult, even contrary to what I wanted from life. When I first started at Cargill, I felt way out of my depth at first. The misalignments that began shortly after I started integrating systems and resources seemed to be signs that maybe I was putting too much pressure on something that wasn't truly meant to be. If I had been quick to judge, I might have missed out on all the opportunities I've had since.

The only appropriate reaction to hardships that form when we've made a big change in life is to simply dig in our heels. It won't do us any good to go about second-guessing the decisions we've made. More often than not, the hardships we experience are a result of the winds trying to change us for the better. And if they didn't, they provided an experience to learn.

Of course, it's hard to ignore them when those decisions are simply contrary to the direction our lives need to take. Many of us feel that one decision we make will forever alter our course. Though there may be serious ramifications that come from making a decision contrary to who you are, no decision lasts forever.

Though there are many times in our lives when a wrong decision seems like the end of the world, it is, perhaps, never truer than when we are young. So many of us think that the relationships we form in high school will last forever. The partner we choose seems like the only one for us, and if those relationships fail, it feels as if there is no one else for us. The career choice we make in high school may seem like the perfect opportunity for us, directed by aptitude tests or the ever-present urging of people who love us, but when we make it out into the real world, sometimes, that decision simply doesn't stick. By the time we experience time alone, truly working on ourselves, the trajectory of our lives may be completely different.

That can be a scary proposition. But there's also something so freeing in it.

We aren't destined to sit in a box. We are destined to take risks and search for so much more.

Those periods when I took significant risks to try something new proved to be some of the most important in my life. But of course, they didn't come without their disadvantages. There were times of pain and disappointment. There were moments of doubt. I think those feelings are universal. They're part of the human experience.

During the most difficult times, I understand the impulse to let pain and disappointment pull you down. Risk is never easy, and those sleepless nights can wreak havoc on what confidence you've developed. But there's so much power when you put on a smile, even in hard times. When in the most difficult positions, sometimes, that positivity is the only thing you can hold on to.

At many times in my life, I borrowed the positivity that kept me going. Friends and family have given me healthy doses of it when life seemed the grimmest. But that positivity is contagious, and there are always ways to pull through.

One of the greatest lessons I've learned working through a risk-riddled life is just how easy it is to remain stress-free. I'm hardly saying that I'm not prone to anxiety, but I've found a purpose beyond that. Focusing on anxiety can pull you down, but even faking a positive attitude, especially in tough times, can guide you toward a purpose that helps you rise above almost anything.

STANDING STRONG

The risks you take sometimes come with unexpected hardships. As much as I would like to say that positivity had complete power over my abilities to adapt, it couldn't cushion me against the significant attacks on my character when I first started at Cargill.

Shortly after my appointment, I started to see some backlash. In particular, one peer of mine seemed awfully vexed when I showed up. Most of the people I worked with of executive status were happy to have me on board, but I couldn't ignore the angry stares that came from one man who, I'd heard, wanted the position I had been awarded.

I was one of the only women around the senior leadership table. Very few women had made it to the top of a global corporation like Cargill, and I quickly found myself, once again, fairly alone. Of course, that feeling wasn't unusual for me. Very few women had made it to executive positions in IT. In fact, it had been so long that I had been among few women that it hardly seemed to faze me anymore. It was just another part of the job.

I wasn't entirely sure what I had done to offend that man. But it seemed like a mission of his to get me out of there as quickly as possible.

It wasn't until about six weeks into my new position that I started to notice a significant problem. It started with simple things. When we would work together, we would agree on our numbers for our presentation, but those numbers would somehow change when we entered a larger meeting. I knew I hadn't changed them, so I would just think quickly to come up with a reason for the shifting numbers. And it kept happening.

Soon, it wasn't just me who was being affected. It seemed like everything he did was geared toward getting me to quit. Some members of my team were starting to feel the strain of trying to keep up with the members of his team. He started approaching people on my team, telling whoever would listen to give me poor feedback. Eventually, an email surfaced, written by him and his team: "Let's get Kim." The contents of the email included messaging about making me look bad. My peer was telling people to do things, say things, that would ultimately reflect badly on me.

It became increasingly surreal. At no other point in my life had I been treated like this by someone else, someone who likely wanted my job. I'd never done anything personally to him before. Yet I was being targeted.

Because I had just started the job, I didn't have any strong supporters. It took the courage of one of my direct reports to inform me about the issues. He approached me with the facts, telling me that what was happening was unethical, and that he wasn't going to continue doing this. He had already reported my peer's bad behavior to HR, but I followed suit, corroborating his findings with the evidence I'd gathered.

I had the last four or five months of his unethical behavior documented. At most companies, it would be more than enough, but he had been there for a long time. He had seniority and a lot more credibility than I did. It would have been well within reason for me to quit the job right then and there. I was being publicly attacked by a team of people, all for the benefit of one person.

But something in me prompted me to stay.

Once the information was out, I felt more isolated than ever. The subversive tactics used previously weren't enough now. He was starting to get more brazen all the time. He and I became embroiled in a six-week investigation, and I was extremely nervous. It was one of the first times in my life that I was truly frightened at work. Though no one had expressly pulled me aside to physically harm me, it didn't stop me from carrying mace with me when I walked to my car.

It took nine months for things to return to normal. My coworker had been let go, but I couldn't help but feel the same antsy feelings I felt during the entire almost two-month investigation. There's a part of me that will never forget the feelings I felt during that time.

Shortly after the incident, my supervisor pulled me aside to tell me that he was surprised I had pushed through everything. It would have been easy to quit. It would have been easy to walk away. But it's not in me to quit. I'm used to being the underdog. I'm used to fighting, to competing harder. It's not in me to settle.

Those events happened over a decade ago, but I still think about them. Though the disastrous events had affected so many people at the time, I hoped I could use them as an opportunity to change some minds. There was a lot of risk involved in staying in that position, but it paid off. The reward of knowing the people I've come to know, of seeing the things I've come to see, was well worth the fight, though it might not have felt that way at the time. This experience taught me that no matter the struggle, if I'm willing to pull through when things get tough, I'll be infinitely more rewarded.

THE REWARD IN RISK

They say, "No risk, no reward," but life often gets more complicated. Taking a step into the unknown is one of the most terrifying experiences in life, especially if it's your first time.

But how can you afford to not take that risk?

We often miss out on so much in life because we're not willing to risk what we have. The first time we step out of the house to do something on our own, the first job we take when we're unsure we're qualified, or the risk of quitting our job to pursue something that we've always wanted to do takes a lot of guts, but they're often the starting points for launching us toward new horizons.

I'm frequently surprised by how many people are desperate to try something new, to risk it all, but are so frightened to try anything outside of what they've done before. In fact, the stress they put upon themselves by rationalizing their reasons for not taking a risk is greater in the long run than if they took the risk anyway. How strange that we box ourselves into a prison of our own making.

Luckily, there are ways to break out of that. Seeing the rewards that come from risk can be a long time in the making, but there are ways to persuade yourself to take that risk anyway.

Taming the Inner Tempest

Stress is one of the leading reasons for putting off following your dreams. What if you don't make it? What if you're not good enough? What if you try but ultimately fail? These questions are soul-consuming, eating away at your willpower with every passing moment wasted on them. The truth is, you'll never completely escape all the stress in life. In fact, your stress might come back two- or threefold when you take a chance. So how do you overcome that?

It all comes down to the message we tell ourselves. That voice inside of us that tells us there's no way we can succeed, there's not enough money in the bank, or what we want to do isn't worth our time lies to us. So, instead of giving it a voice, silence it.

Let's do a brief thought experiment. Think about the time you spent today: How much time did you spend at work, sleeping, eating, doing your hobbies, or engaging in mindless scrolling on your phone? Often, the time we think we spend embroiled in something worthwhile turns out to be a distraction from what we can become.

Break free from the cycle by weighing your options. Think of every action you do as something that's taking you away from something else. Then, own the actions. We often leave a lot of peace of mind on the table because we're committed to becoming more self-conscious about our actions. But what if we weren't? What if, instead of questioning the reward we could get from the risk taken, we simply chose to be happy?

The difficult times will always find us. But that doesn't mean we can't remain positive through those experiences. Sometimes, if nothing else, that's the greatest reward of all.

Calculated Chaos

It's easy to get bogged down in life by the daily choices we have to make. We often take on so much more than we should have to handle. We want to do everything, hold every responsibility. For some of us, it's easier to just take the reins. But that usually means putting off risk.

How many times have you said no to something exciting, something new, simply because you put so much on your plate that you can't make room for anything else? We often deprive ourselves of some of the greatest rewards we could ever receive because it's too difficult to turn something down.

I often encourage those who come to me with these challenges to take a closer look at their lives. Rather than wearing every hat at once, be intentional about where your responsibilities lie—and even more intentional about when you take them on. Find a balance that feels sustainable, and recognize when it's time to set something down before its weight becomes overwhelming.

It almost seems strange, giving advice like this, thinking about how many hours I've spent simply existing in chaos because everything needed to be done in a certain way, and I felt I was the most qualified person to do it. It's been one of the most difficult lessons I've had to learn, but it's also the most valuable. The risks I've taken in life, risks that have yielded incredible rewards, have only come about because I was able to create a balance where initially there was none. The rewards wouldn't have been nearly as sweet had I not first considered how to balance my life.

Fortune Through Bold Moves

When was the last time you trusted your gut in any risky venture? There are so many people telling you to Google every aspect of your life. Is it safe to change jobs in this economy? Is it wise to talk to your partner about how you're feeling, or should you just keep everything bottled up inside? Should you take the chance to invest in something you're truly passionate about?

The internet doesn't have all the answers, though many people online would like to think it does. Most situations are unique and highly dependent on people and circumstances. Sometimes, the best solution is to develop a fully intentional mindset and give 100 percent to what our gut tells us.

So, what is your gut telling you to do?

Those gut decisions often come with a healthy helping of faith. It's best not to overthink any of the decisions you make. No decision is final. Few changes are fatal. You're never required to stick with a decision you made at the moment, so why not take that chance?

If timing is the issue, this is your sign to stop waiting and wishing. There will never be a completely perfect time. Circumstances will never perfectly line up. Sometimes, that reward is right around the corner, waiting for you to gain courage.

There is infinitely more to gain from taking a chance than from standing by and overthinking.

Who knows how your life could change? Who knows how much you could truly grow?

A PERSONAL RISK

How do we take advantage of risk? To perhaps put things in perspective, it's time we choose risks that will build us up.

Some years ago, when I was still working at Target, I had the opportunity to talk to many people about improving their careers. It became something of a passion of mine to help people along. I had been given so much, so it only made sense to give back. One of the most common stories I heard involved creating a professional mask. To many, it seemed so much easier to accept and shoot for risks if their personal lives were separate from their professional ones.

Though this method of coping is extremely common, it highlights an imbalance that eventually leads to burnout. It becomes extremely taxing to create one persona for your personal life and another for your business life. But some believe it's the only way to move forward with professional risk.

On one more recent occasion, I had the opportunity to speak to a man named Bill. Bill had two young kids, and he was struggling to find a balance between the demands of work and being a father. He confided in me that it was extremely difficult to manage the two. It felt like he had to leave a part of himself behind every time he went to work. He would give all that he could, sometimes sacrificing his personal life, just so he could succeed at work. He was providing for his family, a noble cause. And one all too familiar.

Bill became a friend. I saw in him the same struggle I had experienced in my first years as an executive.

During an especially busy week, Bill and I were expected to show up to a meeting with a supervisor. Bill was gone at the time. He had taken a vacation, his first in a long time. When we were informed of the meeting, Bill had told me he could make it, even if that meant he had to sacrifice some vacation time with his family.

It was one of the first times I had ever been frustrated with Bill. He had already been struggling to maintain a work–life balance. Before we could prep for the meeting, I simply told him to focus on his family. There would be enough time in the future for him to make up for that meeting. The most important thing in life wasn't his work or his coworkers. With his attention already so divided, it was time to focus on what really mattered. I had gone through the same thing. I had focused too much on the things that never really mattered. If I could set Bill on the right track early, it would be worth it.

I wouldn't be where I am now if it weren't for the risks I've taken. Perhaps one of the most important risks was to set aside time for the people in my life. Instead of needing to focus entirely on work, to build my personal empire through advancement and my accomplishments, I needed to spend time with the people who matter most. At the end of the day, those are the people I've chosen to live my life with. Those are the people who've seen me grow, cry, and succeed. They're the most valuable risks I've ever taken.

It's funny to me, years later, to look back at where I might have been if I had focused entirely on work. Surprisingly, the risk I took by becoming my true self, by taking off that professional mask and living my authentic self every day, turned out to be my most lucrative decision. The people at work saw a new me. I've reached far more people by living authentically than I ever would have if I'd failed to create that balance.

Prioritizing the right things was a risk. But if I had overthought my decision to take a step back from work, who knows where I would be today? I am who I am because of those risks. I've succeeded only because I insisted on being happy.

9

Climbing Without Ceilings

INGE IBS

At the turn of the millennium, I felt myself starting to slow down. I never like to think of myself as someone who stopped moving, but every day seemed to show a new limitation. The blessings of old age had come with downsides. Instead of visiting my grandchildren, I found many of them had to come to me. Helping people meant inviting them into my home, but I started getting frequent headaches, pains that I couldn't explain. I'd never been someone who easily fell ill, but it seemed like those pains were increasing with every passing week. They were never something I complained about. Everyone around me had such full lives, and I didn't want anyone to worry about me. Besides, I had Fritz, and we could manage. I had been lucky thus far to live as long as I had.

I started to live vicariously through my loved ones. They were having new adventures, exciting lives, and I felt like I was part of them based on their colorful stories. It was like I was living whole lifetimes without ever having to leave my home.

Kimmy was just starting her life. She had married a wonderful man and soon had children of her own. I could hardly believe I was a great-grandmother. She came to visit me often, and we had weekly phone calls and letters. She had so much on her plate. She was doing so much, taking so little time for herself.

In my mind, I still saw that little girl growing up on my farm, and I missed those days. Many of those days were so carefree. It concerned me how much she was putting on herself. I had done the same thing myself. It's that German background. Part of me felt glad that she carried many of the genes that Fritz and I hoped to pass on to future generations, but it all comes with a cost. I saw so much of myself in Kim. I started to worry that, maybe, she was pushing herself too much.

Kimmy always had ambitions. She always wanted to exceed her bounds, explore new things, break through boundaries. There's much to be said about that kind of lifestyle, but it's easy to become lost.

It had taken me a long time to realize that one of the most important things I could ever achieve was the simplicity of a farm built with your own hands. Perhaps, at one point, I might have wished that I could have succeeded in the way my father did before the war. We had wanted for nothing, and that beautiful, large house set the stage for such beautiful memories, some of the only ones that I have of my homeland.

But the life I had created with Fritz and my small family had grown exponentially. I never stopped working, but I loved the challenge. I found in that simple life a balance I couldn't have found anywhere else. Though I was at peace, I was worried that Kim was moving too far away from that.

Her first decade of married life was tough. No life is completely simple. But I watched her from afar, deeply proud of her. I frequently sent her messages containing scriptures or quotes, things that I thought could help her through some of those difficult problems. And I always had a prayer in my heart for her to achieve balance.

Soon enough, I saw a change. Though she was stubborn, she had found a way to bring more balance into her life. Maybe that trait ended up being a blessing after all. I couldn't believe the things that Kim was doing. She had always shown potential, but now, she was growing in international influence, something I could never have hoped to achieve. Yet the details were so vivid. Listening to Kim talk about her life working internationally seemed almost like a dream from the past. She would tell me about her travels to some of the most beautiful places in the world.

Then, she told me of her visits to Russia and Bulgaria.

Something inside of me still had me in its grasp. I found it hard to keep an open mind when hearing about those cultures. Kim talked about them with such enthusiasm, but a part of me was still trapped in 1948. I still remembered what the Soviet Union had done to my beloved country, though Russia hadn't been Communist for more than a decade. I still remembered the war-torn cities. I still remembered the faces of desperation.

I hadn't realized I still struggled with this. I thought I had put it behind me long ago. I had forgiven, but I just couldn't seem to forget.

But perhaps something new was dawning. It had been a lifetime since the war. I imagined the faces of the people Kim told me about. I imagined the smiles and the frowns, so similar to my own. It was like there was a new world out there.

I didn't notice myself walking slowly out the door. I looked over the old farm, so much more vacant than it had ever been before. I knelt down, setting an old, wrinkled hand down to the earth and pulling up a handful of dirt. I had found so much joy in the beautiful Minnesota countryside, and I felt a sense of gratitude for a life that had prioritized a connection to the earth. Those people, tens of thousands of miles away, felt the same yearnings I did. We had all come so far. For the first time in a long time, I felt truly connected to all the people across the Atlantic.

And I smiled.

A WORLD WAITS BEYOND

I often find that as situations change, people like to stay the same. It's easy to do less, accept the minimum. That kind of mindset leads us to a rut, perpetually engaging in the same activities, regardless of the effects it might have on our mental or physical health. It's difficult to make that change, but I always have one message for the people who are looking to improve their lives: Don't settle.

After I had worked at Cargill for nearly a decade, I felt like there was a part of me that needed to change. I always felt like I had a purpose-driven mission, and it was important to me to make sure that I was following my passions and staying true to myself. So, when I received an invitation to join Cencora, I gladly accepted.

The transition wasn't as stark as it may have appeared on the outside. Cencora was a Fortune 10 company, and it led a global team. The company had a lot of the characteristics I had loved so much at Cargill. But what really attracted me to the company was the collaborative and entrepreneurial spirit.

How many companies truly have the goal of making sure everybody wins? Cencora wanted its team to be the best, just like I did. It wanted clear lines of communication that let everyone know their role in their team. Its forty-six thousand employees all had the goal to win together. We each wanted to help each other, and this allowed me to uphold more than one of my pillars: community and work.

I took the position of senior vice president of global business services. I was brought in to stand up shared services, the same assignment I had spent years doing at Cargill. I optimized, bringing efficiency. It was like an extension of myself. I had spent so much time learning how to be productive in my personal life—things such as clearing my mind with yoga, keeping my household in line, meeting each day with a smile—that it seemed like such a natural progression. Perhaps that's what Cencora saw in me. It made such a natural fit.

But the new position also brought other factors into the mix. I had a new culture to learn, new relationships to build.

I had developed a playbook for success at Cargill. I had spent so much time working with so many people across the globe that I had amassed documents about what worked and what didn't. I wasn't sure what experience I could leverage or couldn't, but when the methods didn't quite line up the way I had expected them to, I was almost surprised when I became a little giddy. Sure, having that knowledge fit exactly into my new position would have been easier, but the mismatch meant that I had the chance to try something new.

It's become apparent to me over the years that my technical skills, although very helpful, aren't the be-all and end-all of my success. One of my greatest skills is adaptability, a skill that only comes about through many years of experience.

I discovered long ago that despite the benefits of remaining in a single position, I needed the opportunity to grow. I needed to stretch muscles I had never used before or grow new skills altogether. I wanted a new assignment. I wanted something that would challenge me. New situations can be stressful, but I'll never regret my chosen path of adaptability.

Recently, a mentee of mine told me about her career. She had been at the same company for sixteen years. Just a few more years, and she could retire from there. Though I never begrudge anyone for choosing to stay in a position that fulfills their needs, I felt like something was missing. She was coming to me for a reason. Something simply wasn't right.

When I pressed her on the issue, she finally opened up to me: Something inside her was telling her to try something new. Perhaps it was the fear of starting over that had stopped her from listening to her inner voice. Perhaps it was merely comfort. When I heard about her dilemma, I couldn't help but smile. "I've been there before," I said. "But I also know that not listening to your gut can lead to a life of regret. If you want to try something new, do it now. There's never a better time to stop settling."

BURNING THE SAFETY NETS

It's a cliché to say that what the elderly always regret are opportunities wasted. But perhaps it's a cliché for a reason. We often find ourselves standing at the edge of a dense, uncharted forest. The trail ahead is faint, the underbrush thick, the shadows stretching long. We convince ourselves the path is too tangled to traverse, too uncertain to follow. Instead of venturing into the unknown, where sunlight filters through the trees, we linger in the clearing or retreat to familiar ground.

But what's waiting on the other side of that unknown? Without that step forward, you'd never be able to answer that enduring question: What if?

When was the last time you thought about what it really means to fight for something? Was it when you felt stuck, like you weren't living up to your potential? Or maybe it was when you found yourself at a crossroads, faced with a choice to take a leap and risk getting hurt or stay where it felt safe. Too often, we settle for "good enough" because we convince ourselves it's better than nothing. But relationships built on a sense of obligation rarely bring happiness. Jobs you take just because they're convenient and familiar don't spark fulfillment. And enduring pain simply because finding a solution seems too hard will only drain your energy and limit what you're capable of in other areas.

Instead of thinking, This is good enough, *what if, instead, you thought,* What can I do that I didn't think I could do?

Many detrimental phrases we tell ourselves keep us from finding something truly extraordinary. Finding friends among people who think differently from you can give you perspectives you never knew existed. Taking a life-changing trip that you were too afraid to take before could change your entire perspective and even the course of your life. Don't let the fear of not making it slow you down.

I always tell people to do as much as they possibly can. You never know if an opportunity in front of you might be a once-in-a-lifetime chance. Why not take that chance? Why not be the first person, or even the only person, to take a risky leap? Start small, but start with *something*.

So, to stop yourself from falling victim to the end-of-life regret that many people experience, take a look at where you're going now. Take a look back at what you've already done in life. If you were to die today, what kind of legacy would you leave? Can you tell yourself you've at least attempted to do everything that you wanted to do? Or will your eulogy be short? Are you truly proud of the life you've lived so far, or are you already regretful of the things that might have been?

At the end of the day, sitting on your couch may be more comfortable, but is it rewarding? You only live once, so why not take advantage of the time you have?

GROWING PAINS

Those sacrifices you make often come with hardships, though. It's like stretching a muscle you've never stretched before, or at least one you haven't stretched often or as far. When you're starting out, you begin to feel the aches after a while.

When I first started at Cargill, I had a lot of unsettled people working under me. There were so many roles that had been switched around, so many changes that had made drastic differences to people's lives, people's occupations. Mentally, I had resigned myself to following through on all the changes we had planned to implement to drive value for the company, even if that was hard to accept for everyone involved. But that's not to say it didn't sting when people were impacted. All in all, I found myself getting a bit overwhelmed at times. Not for the first time, and certainly not for the last, I started to wonder if I had taken the right calculated risk.

I became acutely aware that I wasn't leading the right team. While everyone on the team was incredibly talented, it wasn't the right team to implement so many of the unique changes at hand. Some of their strengths just didn't quite align with what we needed. The only way to help was to start building another team. I needed to make some shifts, some alterations.

So, shortly after a major career change, I orchestrated a serious revamping of my new team.

I approached the organization's transformation with a strategic mindset, making thoughtful changes while keeping what could stay intact. Throughout the process, I focused on creating an environment where people could thrive, ensuring the journey remained both productive and enjoyable. Along the way, I built lasting connections with incredible colleagues—many of whom I still stay in touch with today. Despite the growing pains, I knew I was making a meaningful impact, and that sense of purpose has stayed with me.

And, as mentioned earlier, nine years after I started at Cargill, I found myself once again leaving my job. Just a week before leaving, I had headed a town hall meeting in Costa Rica for my team of 1,600 people. The people who had grown with me filled that auditorium with smiling faces. The coworkers I had known for years, people I considered friends, all met to give me a plaque to commemorate what I had done to help build the team. We recognized the powerful brand we had created together.

But, more than that, we were meeting to say goodbye for the last time.

It was a special yet emotional day. There, in the beautiful country of Costa Rica, we celebrated just one of the eight locations around the world that we had built and were really proud of.

But the accomplishments were hardly just about monumental buildings. We had all grown together. My team made me a video with all the pictures of things we had done together over the years. I received a lot of handwritten notes and cards. The smiling faces around me seemed like my legacy. The true reward I had received wasn't the beautiful plaque but the happiness of the people who had come to see me.

It's hard to imagine my life now without experiencing a global network. It's so much a part of me to include different cultures and different ways of thinking in my leadership. My knowledge about the world is far more valuable for my leadership than anything I could read in a book. It's one of those life lessons that you just can't get anywhere else.

So, would it have been easier to stay? Quite possibly. But I don't want to just settle on the good times I had in the past. I'll always love the people that I've worked with, but the question is, how many other experiences like that can I have? By not settling, it means I'm still on a journey. And I can't wait to see what's around the next corner.

THE PRIVILEGE OF TRYING

How often do we complain and tell ourselves that it's just too hard to try something new? If we're honest with ourselves, it's one of the most common excuses out there. It's what stops us from progressing.

But there's truly no reason to stop, no reason to settle on anything. There is always space to grow.

It's striking to me how privileged we all are to live in a place where we can consistently learn. We have the freedom to explore anything we'd like, and it's never too late to start.

Even if it's just for a few minutes a day or an hour, there's always a little time in the day to improve yourself.

It may be unconventional, but one of my greatest motivators is the passage of time. Rather than dwelling on the years behind me, I focus on the finite years ahead. There's still plenty of time to accomplish what matters, but not an unlimited amount—and that reality fuels me. It reminds me that simply having the chance to try is a privilege. Motivation is out there for anyone willing to look inward—all it takes is a little reflection.

Living for Impact

So many of us are in an advantaged position. Though it might not seem like it at certain points in time, there is always a little wiggle room to try something new, to look for something different. So, the first question you have to ask yourself is this: How can I spend a little bit of that wiggle room on someone else?

Taking your eyes off yourself and focusing on someone else is one of the best ways to recognize not only how much you have but also how much you can change. It gives you a bird's eye view from someone else's perspective.

I was exceptionally lucky to have my grandmother as an inspiration. Yes, as she got older, I did my best to take care of her, but she did so much more for me than she probably realized. As soon as I took my eyes off myself, I realized I couldn't settle for a life without helping other people. It's the legacy she left that I only hope I can uphold.

At the end of the day, the thing that really matters is other people. All monumental buildings crumble away eventually. All accomplishments are ultimately lost to the sands of time. But the small things we do for other people impact them for the rest of their lives. And it's possible that the example you leave behind will be picked up by someone who values your mission just as much as you did.

The Stories That Ignite Change

More than five hundred years ago, a boy had the dream to fly. It had never been done before, and people believed that it was only for the birds. But that boy believed that one day, in some way, someone would figure it out. Perhaps it would be him. Throughout his sixty-seven years of life, he had the idea of flight heavy on his mind. He dissected the theories of aerodynamics by studying birds. He became fascinated with anatomy, ultimately drawing some of the most influential art pieces of all time. But at the end of his life, he was never able to devise a device that would allow humans to fly.

Four hundred years later, two brothers turned the dream into reality by building the first flying vehicle. Their inspiration? The man who devoted his life to the idea of flight but couldn't bring it to fruition himself—Leonardo da Vinci. Though he never saw his vision take off, da Vinci's relentless pursuit of the impossible ignited a spark that would burn through the centuries, fueling those who finally achieved what he could only imagine.

I have always believed in the idea of embodying the best qualities of those who are gone. Continuing and leaving a legacy is one of the most important things that we can accomplish in life. It shows that we've done something, been someone. But, perhaps more importantly, it shows what we respect and love about the people who came before us.

Not settling often comes from the inspiration of others. Who you can be isn't set in stone. Though you think you have your own limitations, many, if not all of them, can be overcome. The stories of the people who inspire you the most don't have to be from long ago. The most powerful inspirations don't have to be from the distant past; in fact, the closer they are to us in time, the better. They show what we've done. They show what we can be.

And someday, because of the incredible life you have lived, someone will use your story as inspiration.

Achieving Your Potential

Do you live up to your potential? I suppose none of us do, really. Especially not those of us who yearn for something greater.

I fear that so many of us waste time on things that never really matter. Many of us leave the incredible stories we could have created in the dust because it's either too difficult or we don't know where to start.

The solution is perhaps one of the most difficult lessons I've ever had to learn. It's why I use it as a launch point for many of my mentees: Be intentional. Instead of spending too much time worrying about what others think of your decisions, actively isolate the feelings that are stopping you from doing what you feel you were always meant to do. Instead of merely turning to your phone to flip through endless videos, actively sit down and plan your future. Instead of convincing yourself to stay in a job you're just settling for, actively seek out new experiences and possibilities that scare you.

I wouldn't say I'm ever fully satisfied with the life I'm living. I always want to grow more, be more, love more. Even so, I know I'm embodying the qualities I admire most of one of the most incredible people I've ever known: my grandmother. In the end, that's one of the greatest accomplishments I could ever achieve.

SAY NO TO NOTHING

At its heart, not settling is about searching for more despite the obstacles. There are things I've yet to try; there are places I've yet to go. I don't have time to slow down.

Since my diagnosis of MS and the COVID-19 pandemic, I've been even more determined to push myself. We never truly know how long we have left on this earth, and there's no point in speculation. It's best to pursue what I want to do in the time I have left. So, just because I'd always wanted to do it, I hiked around Iceland, traveled to Australia, and went horseback riding in Costa Rica.

Hiking in Iceland isn't for the faint of heart. It has treacherous terrain and a sweeping volcanic landscape that makes for uneven footing. But it's also one of the most beautiful places in the world, and I wanted to see it for myself.

Giving in to the symptoms of my MS would be the easy choice. Settling is definitely an easier path for most of us. But again, it's not in me to quit. If I want to do something, I can find a way to make it happen, despite any physical or mental setbacks.

Why should you live a life on the ground when you can soar?

10

Shattering the Facade

INGE IBS

The pain in my head was becoming more frequent all the time.

It seems that with age, what you gain in wisdom, you lose in physical ability. Though I didn't bother going to the doctor frequently, I knew I needed some help. I had passed eighty, eighty-five. I found myself quickly reaching ninety years. My doctor told me I had myopathy. It wasn't so surprising, perhaps. But it was becoming increasingly burdensome. I frequently woke up stiff, massaging spasms out of my muscles. And by the time I had reached my late eighties, I could no longer stand.

Kimmy still came to visit me often, which was a blessing, considering I could no longer make my way around as easily. Every time she visited, I could see a pang of worry on her face. "Don't worry," I said. "It's not hereditary. It's not MS." But every time, the smile she gave me never quite reached her eyes.

I never considered myself down-and-out. As age weakened my body further, I committed myself to that same philosophy. There were still things I could do around the house, chores I could complete, and people I could visit—or, perhaps more correctly, they could visit me. And my house would remain a home.

And I wouldn't let my mind succumb to the problems of age. There were still plenty of things I could do to stay sharp. I memorized the names of the people in my family, contemplating the memories all the time. I still wrote regularly. I still spoke with my husband every day. Though my body was dwindling, my mind never would.

But the headaches were becoming worse. Perhaps they were nothing.

As those Minnesota days came and went, I became ever more aware of how beautiful it all was. I could no longer stand, work the ground I had lived on for so many years, but perhaps that didn't matter. It was an incredible revelation to me. There's something quite beautiful in hard work, in a simple life. Perhaps it wasn't the life I would have chosen for myself when I was young. But it had turned into something far more fantastic than I could have ever imagined.

After turning ninety-one, I understood that I should do something about those headaches. I had dealt with them for ten, fifteen, perhaps twenty years. But with a body so incapacitated already, it was perhaps time I found out what was really wrong.

My doctor took me in for a brain scan. They told me it would be much easier to find out what was wrong if they had a clear picture.

When I returned to my room, I sat, hands folded, waiting for the results. Fritz was with me, silent but patient by my side as we waited together. I don't know what I really expected. A part of me wished for some immediate relief, something that would make sense of my continual headaches over the years. Another part of me wondered what would happen if something was actually wrong. Maybe there was peace in not knowing.

When my doctor returned, his face looked grim. There was a lump in my head. Cancer.

At first, I was shocked, but it quickly faded to serenity. At least I knew.

"We can try to remove it," he said.

I took a deep breath and steeled myself for the response. I turned to Fritz, giving him a genuine smile. "No," I said. "I think I've lived long enough."

We'd been together long enough that I'm sure Fritz already knew the answer I was going to give. It couldn't have been easy seeing your companion for the better part of a century accepting a difficult fate, but he bore it just for me. A mercy.

Over the next couple of days, I let my family know the news. It was tempting to shed tears, but I wanted something more than that. Reaching the age of ninety-one was worth celebrating, and the people around me were worth celebrating with. I wouldn't fade into death with tears. I wanted a celebration.

Two weeks seems such a short time to know you have left. But I didn't need to live a life in those two weeks. I had already lived a life I was more than proud of. I was surrounded by the people I loved the most. And I was waiting for a bright future after passing through this life into the next. I knew, when I closed my eyes for the last time, I had lived a life of gratitude. I had lived a life of being true to myself. And I had seen the people I loved the most grow in ways I could never have imagined.

Even in a life of struggle and sorrow, I wouldn't change a thing.

DISCOVERING THE TRUE GOAL

Sometimes, it's hard to pull myself away from hard times. I look at the life of a woman who did so much, was so proud of all she had accomplished. Looking back at my own life, many times, it seemed like a mishmash of adrenaline and rapid decision-making. If I didn't have the benefit of hindsight, I might think I wasn't working toward a true goal, merely a future with a promising brightness.

Back at the beginning of my career, in the days when my kids were young, I did everything I could to make our situation work. I was going to school to get my MBA, working full-time, and mothering two small boys. Getting through the day was difficult, so I came up with strategies to make my life a little bit easier.

It can be a nightmare to get kids ready in the morning with a busy schedule. I figured I would skip the desperate rush with a brilliant plan. The night before, when I put my kids to bed after their baths, instead of pajamas, I put them in their clothes for the next day. It was a strategy that saved me hours in the long run.

But I can't say I didn't get strange looks from the other moms.

Not only was I one of the only mothers who ushered kids not entirely quaffed for the day, but I was also the one absent at most parent meetings. As I became more involved in my kids' lives, I became acutely aware of my lack of acceptance into the school's "Moms' Club." Other moms volunteered for school events. They made elaborate desserts for school celebrations. They even chitchatted outside of school hours with each other, discussing playdates and the struggles of being a mom. It's a club I could never enter into because I simply didn't have the time.

I remember those mornings of being the first mother to drop off my kids and the last to pick them up later. I remember the times when it seemed like the parents who had it all together talked about me behind my back. Sometimes, it was difficult to assuage the guilt that came from not behaving perfectly in line with the norm.

But then, it was always apparent that I wasn't normal. I had known from an early age that "things" never really mattered to me. I never needed to have the fanciest car or the most expensive clothes. It was simply not who I was, and it's not who I've turned out to be.

STEPPING OFF THE HAMSTER WHEEL

It's hard to pull ourselves away from the pull of material possessions. Often, when life is going well, we catch ourselves yearning for what someone else has—their car, their home, or their lifestyle. But in chasing after these possessions, we risk losing touch with who we truly are.

I've seen so many people fall into the same trap. A lawn that's not mowed at the same rate as the neighbor's can create a panic attack when we're far too invested in what everyone else has in life. An emphasis on wealth can create a shallowness that's difficult to crawl out of. Everyone is looking for the new thing, the new way to appear affluent. But is the shiny sports car really necessary for personal satisfaction or professional success?

At the end of our lives, we all look for the people who love us. On their deathbed, nobody has said they'd rather have spent more time at work.

But I'm constantly surprised by how many people remain chained to their jobs, desperately trying to earn another bonus, to reach another title at the expense of their quality of life.

When we're not on the clock, any disappointment we may feel is often drowned out by the noise of something else. Doomscrolling is the Band-Aid for depression. Anxiety about the future can be curtailed briefly by a funny YouTube video. But the more time we spend glued to the screen, the more we lose a piece of ourselves.

The smallest details of who we are often go unnoticed. The simple joy of running might get overshadowed when we finally have the means to buy those really expensive sneakers. The joy we feel in caring for an elderly relative might be diminished when we're criticized for missing an annual board event. The solace we take in solitude might be interrupted when there's constantly a blaring device near us. It's easy to push aside what we love about ourselves when we're constantly distracted.

The artificial diversions are so tempting. Nearly everything, at some time or other, is competing for our attention. When we're too busy staring at a screen, we lose something about ourselves.

The truth is that we don't need all those other things. A blissful life lies on the other side of peace of mind.

And the solution is relatively simple: gratitude.

I've found that keeping a list, whether physically or in my head, helps me keep things in perspective. As someone with MS, I realize that, one day, I might lose the use of my limbs entirely. But today is not that day, and I can be grateful for that. I could have let the pursuit of worldly gains take me away from a happy life and loving people. But I have the people I care about the most surrounding me during difficult times, and I'm thankful for that too.

When I gain perspective, it's easy for me to see myself as I truly am, not defined by what I can get. Looking back now, I've been blessed with the chance of disappointment. I've been pushed toward the right path and pulled away from the wrong one through trial and error and pain.

Life isn't easy, but who would want it to be? Some of the most difficult parts of my life weren't solved through immediate relief. The times I had to fight through to find out who I really was, forgetting what everyone else was saying, were the times I grew the most. And I learned what I was really made of.

EMBRACING UNEXPECTED GROWTH

When I first started out in my career, I was nearly obsessed with getting the right answer. I overprepared. I stressed way too much over the things that never really mattered. Looking back now, I wonder if it was really a point of pride for me or if it was simply anxiety and perfectionism. But in the moment, it seemed vitally important to prove myself.

Those personal struggles have taught me something quite unique. It was always in my nature to do the most I could to provide as much value as I could. But I started to realize the importance of relaxing on the job. After a while, it didn't seem quite so important to be the first one in the boardroom. It didn't seem quite so important to make sure that my presentations were perfectly scripted.

It's one of those problems that I see most business owners or high-achieving people have: They want to make sure that everything is perfect. It's hard to let go when you've created something and put your heart and soul into it. But, sometimes, that's the right move to make.

Just recently, I mentored a young woman who was starting her own coffee business. She was bright, energetic. She wanted to make the most out of every opportunity she was given, and she excelled because of that attitude. In fact, she had risen from a solopreneur to a business owner with employees. She'd become remarkably successful in a short amount of time.

But that kind of quick success often comes with its own problems. She expected so much of herself, and she hoped that her employees would exhibit the same energy. Unfortunately, she had a low performer working on the team. She wanted to give that person every chance to succeed, but it simply wasn't paying off. As a new business owner, she wasn't entirely sure how to handle the situation.

As I reflected on my experiences, I realized the importance of providing clear, constructive feedback to help others grow. There was a time when I took on more work because I hadn't empowered my team. I learned that having open, honest conversations helped both my team and me reach our full potential.

Developing others through feedback became a crucial skill, allowing me to focus on bigger goals and contribute more effectively to the business. I had to learn that giving feedback meant I was elevating my other employees. I didn't want a single person to take down the work others had built up. Teams need to perform as a unit, and if I was too busy keeping an eye on one person, no one else could fully succeed.

This sweet young woman had a hard time with the concept. She wanted to make her business better, but those difficult conversations are never easy. Nonetheless, she left our discussion with the determination to make a change.

It's often surprising to me how little we expect from ourselves. The power we have to make a difference is always with us if we're willing to stretch our muscles.

That conversation opened my eyes to just how much I've shaped my true self. It's often those moments that we think are the most difficult to overcome that do the true shaping, the true molding. I saw myself in that young woman who was just starting out. I had come so far.

And looking back now, I'd never trade those difficult moments for who I've become.

BECOMING WHO YOU WERE MEANT TO BE

Those difficult moments provide the milestones I need to ensure that I'm becoming who I was meant to be. Those lines on my face are milestones.

Looking at the society we live in, the desperate attempt to hold on to youth often perplexes me. So many people are obsessed with the idea of postponing the wrinkles on their faces and forever looking for the fountain of youth. But why? That's not to say that I wouldn't like to have the health of youth, but if it's a choice between maintaining my wisdom with my age and losing it all for youth, I would choose the wrinkles every time.

I worry that, perhaps, too many of us are whiling away time on things that don't force us to grow. The hard work that comes from starting a family, creating a business, or making a lifestyle change often causes gray hair. In the moment, it can be tempting to want to avoid hardships altogether. But what would become of us if we did?

Becoming who we're meant to be is a journey. It's difficult, and it's challenging. But anything worth having is rarely easy.

Starting with Hope

Starting a career and a family at the same time is enormously stressful. I can't count the mornings I got up feeling like the days before had been a blur. I had to keep it together for my children, my husband, and my job. On some of the toughest days, I truly felt the crush of pressure.

But in those times of despair, I could look forward to a hopeful future. What I was going through at that moment wouldn't last forever. I was building something greater. I was becoming something better.

When you're striving for something that feels impossible, the small steps you take in the right direction can feel so insignificant that it seems like they make no difference at all.

It's at those moments that hope becomes essential. When you give up on yourself, you're letting your future self down. The promise of something brand new, something greater than you could have ever imagined, created through hard work, can push you through nearly anything. The tough times are only temporary.

Hope often gets a bad rap, but it's something that has catapulted me to success over the years. Thinking positively instead of letting the negative ideas cloud my mind has helped me push through.

Putting in that backbreaking work is worth it once that child who was once inside you wishes upon a star. We can make it through anything when we simply accept the possibilities.

Avoiding the Pitfalls of Comparison

"Comparison is the thief of joy" is a saying often attributed to Theodore Roosevelt. So many of us want to become something we're not simply because we've seen someone else do it. Though we've never been particularly interested in gardening, perhaps we want to have a fully landscaped front yard because the neighbor across the street has one. Though we've always wanted a quiet life, we might start to yearn for fame because the lives of those on social media seem so much easier. There's a never-ending stream of ways other people want you to live your life. Falling into that trap can make you miserable.

But the tides requesting your constant attention are sometimes difficult to overcome. It's easy to glance down and respond to just that first email. It's overly tempting to take a look at that short video. It's tantalizing to scroll through Instagram. But those things that are vying for your attention force you to compare them with what you're currently doing. Soon enough, you might find yourself feeling less prepared, less active, or less attractive than the people you see on your screen.

If you find yourself deeply entrenched in these habits, take a major step back. Turn off your phone for the day. Step away from your computer when you're feeling overly stressed. Turn off the TV and go read something instead. Soon enough, you'll find that the quiet moments are the best at helping you identify who you really are.

Accepting Who You Are

And to those who find it difficult to take that moment of silence, simply remember that none of us is alone. It's so easy to succumb to all the pressures surrounding us at every moment. But how would you feel if you could let all of that go?

Occasionally, I'll hear a friend of mine tell me about a steady stream of fad diets. By the law of averages, it would seem that at least *one* of them would work. Whenever they speak to me, they're filled with such hope. Maybe this is the time.

As someone who has struggled with athletics-induced eating disorders in the past, I understand the desire to constantly better yourself. It's easy to think that you're not enough. To many of us out there, we have felt the stinging pain of looking in the mirror and not liking what we see.

But, if we follow that thought to its conclusion, it's easy to see the faults in a plan of perfectionism in physical improvement. If you're not skinny enough, you'll constantly be losing weight until there's nothing left to lose. If your teeth aren't straight enough, you may go through procedures that cost thousands of dollars and be left instead with dentures. There is no such thing as perfection, and it's easy to get lost in trying to achieve the impossible.

So, what if you looked in the mirror and instead decided to love what you saw?

We can never become our true selves if we don't accept where we are. Of course, there's always room for improvement, but it should come from a loving perspective. Grow because you want to improve, not because you hate what you see.

BECOMING

Over the past few years, international travel has become riskier. MS has compromised my immune system, which means that it's easier for me to get sick. It's something I constantly face. But I'm grateful for every day I have the agency and ability to do what I want.

Recently, my niece and her boyfriend, Jon, came to Minnesota to visit his mother. They had the chance to stop by our house for the holidays and share in our celebrations. Jon was chatty, open. Soon enough, I found out that his mother, a fifty-seven-year-old woman, had been diagnosed with MS in her twenties. The picture he painted wasn't a rosy one: She was always sick, and though she hadn't yet reached the age of sixty, everyone in their family felt as though the end was in sight. He was simply grateful to spend as much time as he could with her before she passed on.

I listened in silence for a time, thinking of just how much things had changed since my own diagnosis. "I've been diagnosed with MS too."

Jon looked shocked when I told him. After seeing his mother struggle so much and for so many years, he confirmed what I'd already suspected: "I never would have guessed from looking at you."

Sometimes, I wonder if we're just a bit too hard on ourselves. I occasionally think about the possibility that I might not have the same physical capabilities in the future that I do now. Maybe I'll never walk or do yoga again. Maybe I'll have to stop my international travel one day.

But that hasn't happened yet.

I'm far from a complete picture. I certainly have the goal to accomplish as much as I can in my life. But perhaps the best thing I can tell myself is to take everything one day at a time.

And there's always hope as long as you try.

Conclusion

How many of us stay in a perpetual state of monotony? How many of us feel stuck? How many of us, through brutal years of hard work and life's constant beatdowns, feel it's impossible to change? It's hard to accept that where you are is where you really want to be.

I hope that anyone going through life struggles gets a boost of courage.

Throughout my career, many people have asked me how I got to where I am today. It only makes sense. I've been exceptionally lucky, but I owe much of my success to persevering through difficult circumstances.

It's the growth I've accepted and striven for despite it all that has given me the unique opportunity to stand where I've stood.

Success comes to those who are willing to put in the effort to exercise discipline in their lives. For me, that meant getting my priorities straight and creating a balance I could maintain. It came down to recognizing who I was and choosing to stay true to myself.

Throughout this book, I've shared lessons I've learned along the way. You've seen how I've lived through circumstances that have helped me strive for my potential. I focused on the possibilities when life brought me down. I learned to recognize my unique strengths and helped others realize theirs. I discovered my priorities and changed when I needed to. I shot for the stars and never settled for second best. I continually learned and strove for risky ventures. I learned to never settle and became my true self along the way. But those hard-fought lessons were only the catalysts for concepts far greater.

To those seeking to learn more from my story, I hope you'll look for the lessons I wrote between the lines.

First, *the misunderstood quality of hope tends to push anyone in the right direction*. Throughout my career, I've found that transformation is possible at any stage. Sometimes, we reach a point in our lives that makes it seem as though we're stuck. The career choice you made in college may have set you on a path that turned out to be inconsistent with who you really are. That one decision we made many years ago could have dictated where we are in life right now, but it doesn't always have to be that way.

I hope you'll take the chance to move on to something new at any stage in your career. It's certainly not worth it to stay in a position where you're not happy. If you've felt the urge to change for quite some time, this is your chance to take the leap. Don't settle, personally or professionally, for a life that's not giving you what you want it to.

Next, *underestimation can be your greatest competitive advantage*. Throughout my life, I have been among the few women in technology. There were times when I felt like I was the only one—the only woman, the only mother—in a room full of people who had far different priorities than my own. To those who find the prospect daunting, I can promise you the challenge is worth it. The changes in perspective you experience are sometimes your greatest assets.

Finally, *the lesson I consider to be the most valuable is maintaining a PMA*. My career has put me in some difficult circumstances. I've been the lead for international teams and have overcome considerable and complex challenges in high-stakes, high-visibility roles. I've seen loved ones wrongfully attacked while all I could do was sit back and watch. I've had to accept my own possible limitations after my diagnosis with MS.

But despite it all, I've seen the value of maintaining that PMA. It's why I have constant reminders of it scattered throughout my house.

The truth is, if you maintain a PMA, anything is possible. You can overcome the impossible.

No one decision is a life sentence. No one detrimental occurrence is a death knell. Your life is completely open and bright when your mind is in the right place.

I took a unique path to writing this book. I found happiness in living a life that is dedicated to family, my career, and expanding my horizons. I was never the one to be happiest living contentedly on a farm. But mine is hardly the only way to live an exemplary life.

To me, one of the greatest examples of a successful life will always be my grandmother. She never had the glitz and glam lifestyle, nor did she want it. Her life was dedicated to service and contentment. Though it's not the life path I took, I consider hers wholly successful.

In the end, I've discovered that life's great experiment comes down to persistence—particularly to the dedication to a positive attitude. You see, it doesn't truly matter where you come from, nor does it matter which path you choose.

An enriching life comes in all shapes and sizes, but only if it is stamped with the letters PMA: Positive Mental Attitude.

About the Author

KIM SKANSON is a dynamic corporate executive with a distinguished career leading global operations and spearheading technology transformations at industry giants such as Travelers, Target, Cargill, and Cencora. Known for her strategic vision, resilience, and ability to drive meaningful growth, she has built a legacy of operational excellence and forward-thinking leadership.

Beyond her corporate accomplishments, Kim is a dedicated yoga teacher who seamlessly integrates mindfulness and balance into both her leadership philosophy and personal life. A former college softball player, she channels the same competitive spirit and determination into her passions—whether coaching baseball, playing ice hockey, or mentoring future leaders.

As a proud mother of three driven young men, Kim understands the art of harmonizing a demanding career, family life, and personal aspirations. Whether traveling the world for work or inspiring young athletes in her community, her unwavering commitment to a positive mindset and collaborative spirit remains at the heart of her success.

Through *Attitude Advantage*, Kim shares the transformative mindset strategies and personal growth principles that have shaped her journey. Her mission is to empower others to embrace the power of perspective, unlock their full potential, and navigate life's challenges with resilience, confidence, and purpose.

www.ingramcontent.com/pod-product-compliance
Lightning Source LLC
LaVergne TN
LVHW091548040926
847245LV00001B/4